utah
celebrity
& local
heroes
cookbook

utah
celebrity
& local heroes
cookbook

Royalties Benefit the Park City
Performing Arts Center

Sheila Liermann & Nancy Reid
Lost Trail Productions

*Lost Trail Productions, Inc.
Post Office Box 6160
Ketchum, Idaho 83340
(208) 726-4460*

*Printed in Salt Lake City, Utah,
United States of America*

*Cover art and interior art by
Anton Rasmussen*

*Cover Photographs. Top to bottom:
Robert Redford, Steve Young, Marie
Osmond, Robert & Heather Urich*

*Book and cover design by
woodland & kopfer design,
Ketchum, Idaho*

ISBN: 0-9649428-0-1

*Lost Trail Productions, Inc. books
are available at special discounts
when purchased in bulk as well as
for fund-raising or educational use.
For details, contact the Sales
Director at the address above.*

*All royalties benefit the
Park City Performing Arts Center,
Park City, Utah.*

10 9 8 7 6 5 4 3 2

table of contents

The arts is the one arena where students learn the feeling part of education. One can read Shakespeare and about Shakespeare to try to understand those characters, but the opportunity to see it performed, learn stage combat, period dance, and something about the politics of the day that shaped the Bard's writing, well, that's where academics come alive. And with any luck, you create an audience for the future.

As education and creative thinking related to it undergo great shifts in the 90s, the arts are expected to play a pivotal role in that transition. The magic of foreign languages can be taught through opera. Understanding rhythm and movement—watching music come to life—can be taught through dance. Mathematics are a part of musical instruction and English comprehension is an element of drama. A complete education revolves around exposing the student to as many ideas in as many art forms as possible.

The Park City Performing Arts Center, a longtime dream of the community, will offer students and residents alike a first class facility to participate in and enjoy the finest performances of dance, theater, and music in the Intermountain West.

When the 1,000-seat high school auditorium is complete, it will host performances of Ballet West, the Utah Symphony, the Utah Opera Company, and others. Those groups will offer workshops and residencies for the students and the community-at-large. Also when completed, patrons can expect to see and hear cutting drama and dance and enjoy music festivals from gospel and blues groups to chamber ensembles. Stand-up comedians, one-man shows, and small Broadway touring companies are all expected to take curtain calls at the facility. The popular Sundance Film Festival plans to use the Center to premiere its special films.

Since our beginnings as a rough and tumble mining town, the performing arts have always been an integral part of Park City. The Dewey Theater and Opera House went up about the same time as the saloons in the late 1800s. And since 1926, the Egyptian Theater has offered movies, music, and drama.

But we have grown and so have our needs. This Performing Arts Center will serve as a stage to showcase the finest performers in the Park City School District and the nation. It is a recipe for transcending the ordinary, and for touching the extraordinary.

Our contributors believe that the arts are the window to the soul, and while we would never disagree, we think the stomach isn't a bad route to take either. The combination of Schubert and sorbet cleanses the palette and stirs the imagination. We hope that after reading the recipes included here, you are inspired to create—in whatever form that takes.

Bon Appetit and Break a Leg!

Teri Orr
Executive Director
Park City Performing Arts Center

fred adams

Fred Adams and his wife, Barbara, conceived the idea for the Utah Shakespearean Festival at a laundromat more than thirty-five years ago. With $1,000 seed money and years of dedication and hard work, they have turned that dream into the masterpiece that is the Utah Shakespearean Festival, held each summer at the Randall L. Jones Theater in Cedar City. Fred, the Festival's executive producer, was named Geneva Steel "Man of the Year" for shaping a nascent theater program into a valuable resource for the entire state. He also teaches, directs, and lectures at Southern Utah University in the theater department.

Tibetan Yak Casserole

13

"I got this recipe from Ron Ranson, a scene designer for the Shakespearean Festival's Adams Theater in the 1980s. Ron and his family drove from California to Cedar City each summer. Once the plays were up and running, our families took turns cooking dinner. This was one of our all-time favorites, and it's easy, too."

½	cup (1 stick) butter
1-2	bunches green onions, finely chopped (include the greens)
1	16-ounce can salted cashews, chopped
½	pound mushrooms, thinly sliced
1	teaspoon curry powder
6	eggs
2	slices wheat bread, buttered and cubed
6	ounces cream cheese, softened and cubed
1	cup milk
	freshly ground pepper

☀ Preheat oven to 375°. Butter a 4-quart casserole dish.

☀ In a large skillet, melt the butter. Add the green onions, cashews, and mushrooms. Cook, stirring often, until cashews are brown. Add the curry powder.

☀ In a separate bowl, whisk eggs, and add the bread cubes, cream cheese, milk, and pepper. Add the cashew-mushroom mixture to the egg mixture. Pour into the prepared casserole.

☀ Bake for 40 minutes, or until the "quiver" is gone out of the center. Serve with buttered, heated flour tortillas. Serves 6-8.

lori adamski-peek

Photographer Lori Adamski-Peek has the rare ability to capture with beauty and meaning the images of our world. Her talents were recognized at an early stage in her career. Even though she had taken only a few photo classes while in college (she holds a degree in applied art and design from California Polytechnic State University), she became the main photographer for the U.S. Ski Team soon after graduating. Since then, Lori's work has appeared in **Newsweek, Sports Illustrated, Outside, Ski, National Geographic** *and other publications. She has covered six Olympic Games for* **Newsweek.** *Lori is currently working as a location photographer and some of her clients include Eastman Kodak, Subaru, and Hind Sportswear. Lori lives in Park City with her husband, Tom, and daughters Devin and Kylie.*

Peak Performance Pudding

"My children love this simple, wholesome recipe. It came from my mom in California, so it is comfort food."

2½	cups non-fat milk
¼	cup granulated sugar
2	tablespoons cocoa powder
3	tablespoons cornstarch
½	teaspoon vanilla extract

☀ Place the milk, sugar, cocoa, and cornstarch in a saucepan, and stirring constantly, cook over medium heat until thickened, about 7 minutes.

☀ Add the vanilla and mix well. Pour the pudding into separate bowls, and chill before serving. Serves 4-6.

nancy allen

*When screen star Nancy Allen spoke her first words to Jack Nicholson in the film **The Last Detail**, it was the quiet launching of a film career that has flourished for over fifteen years. Starring roles in **Carrie** and **Blowout** followed and Nancy's performances have consistently received salvos, even from the toughest critics. Nancy played Anne Lewis in **Robocop**, a huge box office success, and in its sequels. Shooting **Touched by an Angel**, brought Nancy to Utah, where she says the people are extraordinarily friendly and the scenery beyond compare.*

Penne Arrabbiata

1	pound penne pasta
2	tablespoons olive oil
3	garlic cloves, minced
1	tablespoon crushed red pepper, about 2 dried chilies
2	cups canned whole plum tomatoes
2	tablespoons chopped Italian parsley
½	cup Pecorino Romano cheese, grated

☀ Place a large pasta bowl in a 300° oven to warm.

☀ Heat the olive oil in a large skillet. Add the garlic and crushed red peppers, and sauté for 1 minute, or until garlic is golden.

☀ Add the tomatoes, breaking them apart as you stir. Cook over low heat for 15 minutes.

☀ Meanwhile, bring a large pot of water to a boil. Add the pasta, and return to a boil. Cook until al dente, about 10-12 minutes. Drain.

☀ Put the pasta in the warmed pasta bowl. Pour the sauce over the noodles. Top with the Italian parsley and grated Romano cheese, and serve immediately. Serves 4.

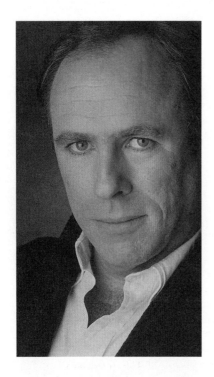

gary armagnac

A dozen years ago, Gary Armagnac drove out of Los Angeles-leaving behind its smog and endless freeways and an evolving screen acting career, including roles in **Star Trek: The Next Generation,** **LA Law,** *and* **TJ Hooker**—*for a life on stage. Gary was the first equity actor to work for the Utah Shakespearean Festival and during his fourteen year tenure he has played many title roles. He has received Hollywood Dramalogue Awards for his Iago in* **Othello,** *Dylan Thomas in* **Dylan,** *and MacBeth in* **MacBeth.** *Gary also serves as the director of education for the Festival at Cedar City's Southern Utah University.*

Farmhouse Cheese Soup

"This soup was originally cooked by my mother at our Pennsylvania farmhouse, where we would go to get away from our New Jersey suburban home. It was also a family favorite during the winter holidays. Cheese soup reminds me of Mom, comfort, good homey smells, family, and my favorite spot in the world—the Pennsylvania farm. Never meant to be low calorie, I tell friends and family when I serve it, 'Hey, life is short. This is comfort food, meant to warm the soul, provide soothing solace, and to stimulate hearty conversation.' I cook for a crowd, so this big batch can be frozen or served as left-overs."

6	stalks celery, chopped
2	large white onions, chopped
4	large carrots, chopped
6	parsnips, chopped
2	large turnips, chopped
6	garlic cloves, minced (or to taste)
8	cups chicken broth
1	cup (2 sticks) butter
	flour as needed to thicken
1	pint half and half
½	pound Gruyere cheese, grated
½	pound Parmesan cheese, grated
	salt and pepper, to taste
	paprika
	Parmesan cheese and croutons, to garnish

☀ In a large pot, simmer the vegetables in the chicken stock until tender, about 20 minutes. Strain, and discard vegetables or save for another use. Reserve the liquid.

☀ Melt the butter in a soup pot over medium heat. Whisk in flour until you have reached a smooth consistency, stirring constantly. Gradually add the cream. Stir in the prepared vegetable stock. Bring to a boil, stirring constantly.

☀ Reduce heat to medium. Gradually add the Gruyere cheese and Parmesan cheese, stirring constantly, until cheeses are melted and well blended. Season with salt and pepper.

☀ Sprinkle with paprika, and serve with croutons, or grated Parmesan cheese sprinkled on top. Serves 12-14.

Most troubled adolescents have discovered the "art" of manipulation. At the Loa-based Aspen Achievement Academy, teens cannot "con" nature. The Academy's fifty-two-day wilderness program brings them face to face with survival in Central Utah's wild and rugged backcountry. In such an environment, students can quickly gain maturity, learn the meaning of self-reliance, and gain a new respect for the care that came so easily at home. Founded six years ago, the Academy is licensed by the State of Utah and employs therapists who work in the field with students, helping them along the path of self-discovery.

Wayne County Baked Beans

Karen Chapel provides this recipe on behalf of the Aspen Achievement Academy. You may use any variety of beans—a medley makes a more colorful dish.

2	pounds ground beef
1-2	onions, chopped fine
½	green pepper, deveined, and chopped fine
1	28-ounce can pork and beans
6	15-ounce cans assorted beans, drained (pinto, great northern, red, black, black-eyed peas, baby lima beans, or kidney)
½-¾	cup molasses
½	cup brown sugar
½	teaspoon dried mustard
¼	teaspoon ground cloves
1	8-ounce can pineapple tidbits (optional)

☀ Preheat oven to 300°.

☀ In a sauté pan, brown the ground beef. Add the onions and green pepper, and cook until soft, about 7-9 minutes.

☀ In a large-capacity casserole or Dutch oven, add the pork and beans, assorted beans, molasses, brown sugar, dried mustard, ground cloves, and optional pineapple. Mix well. Blend in the ground beef, onions, and green pepper.

☀ Cover the casserole or Dutch oven, and bake for 2 hours, stirring occasionally. Check frequently to see if the mixture is dry; you may need to add water. Remove the cover for the last 15 minutes of baking. Serves 40 at a western-style cookout.

dick bass

In 1969, Dick Bass began turning the dramatic landscape around the Little Cottonwood Canyon into what is now Snowbird, a $150 million ski and summer resort. Snowbird's architecture and environmental designs have earned it numerous awards and the honor of being one of the nation's premier resorts. In 1985, Dick completed another personal goal. He became the first person to scale the highest peak on each of the seven continents, and at the same time, became the oldest person, at the age of fifty-five, to climb Mount Everest. He wrote about those experiences in his book, **Seven Summits.** *Always aspiring, Dick sees the future of Snowbird on an even grander scale with more lifts and ski terrain, a performing arts theater, and the development of the Snowbird Institute into a "renaissance center" dedicated to the development of the body, mind, and spirit.*

Gorgonzola Stuffed Filet Mignon

6	filets mignons, about 7-ounces each, about 2-inches thick
12	ounces Gorgonzola cheese
6	slices bacon, hickory smoked is preferred
1	pinch salt
1	pinch fresh ground pepper

Sauce:

2	shallots, minced
1	sprig fresh thyme
1	bay leaf
1	cup red wine
1¼	cups demi-glaze (you may substitute beef stock)
2	tablespoons unsalted butter
1	tablespoon minced fresh parsley
1	tablespoon minced fresh tarragon
1	tablespoon lemon juice
1	pinch cayenne pepper

☀ Set oven to broil.

☀ Place the Gorgonzola cheese in a bowl, and lightly mash with a fork until smooth. Put the cheese in a pastry bag with a small, round tip.

☀ With a boning or paring knife, starting in the middle, put a slit in the edge of the steak. Cut with the knife until you hit two o'clock and then cut left until nine o'clock. Stuff each filet with 2-ounces cheese by placing the tip of the bag inside the hole and squeezing lightly. When finished, wrap each filet with a slice of bacon and secure with a tooth pick. Sprinkle with salt and pepper.

☀ To prepare the sauce: Simmer the shallots, thyme, bay leaf, and red wine until reduced by three-fourths. Add the demi-glaze, and simmer for 15 minutes. Add the butter, whisking lightly. Strain and return the red wine sauce to the pan. Stir in the parsley, tarragon, lemon juice, and cayenne pepper. Keep warm until ready to serve.

☀ Broil the filet mignon for about 3½-4 minutes per side for rare meat, and about 5 minutes per side for medium.

☀ Serve the filet mignon topped with sauce, and your favorite potatoes and vegetables. Serves 6.

stacey bess

No Name Taco Salad

1	pound lean ground beef
1	15-ounce can kidney beans with liquid
1	envelope taco seasoning
1	8-ounce bottle Light Thousand Island Dressing
1	head iceberg lettuce, washed, drained, and torn into bite-size pieces
2	cups Cheddar cheese, grated
1	8-ounce can chopped olives, drained
2-3	tomatoes, chopped
3	cups tortilla chips, broken into bite-size pieces
8	tortilla bowls, available in Mexican food section of most supermarkets
	avocado, sour cream, or salsa, for garnish

✳ In a large skillet, brown the ground beef, about 8 minutes. Drain and discard the liquid. Add the kidney beans with liquid, taco seasoning, and Thousand Island Dressing, and heat through.

✳ In a large bowl, combine the lettuce, Cheddar cheese, olives, tomatoes, and tortilla chips. Add the beef mixture, and stir.

✳ Serve immediately in the tortilla bowls. May garnish with avocado, sour cream, or salsa. Serves 8.

kurt bestor

Visual sound.

The art of giving voice to image.

Such is the work of Kurt Bestor—

composer, arranger, and performer.

He and fellow composer Sam

Cardon won an Emmy for their

compositions for ABC's 1988 Winter

Olympics coverage. Kurt has created

more than twenty feature film

scores, like that of the award-

winning soundtrack to **A More**

Perfect Union. *He is also known*

for conducting and performing

around the country in sold-out

concert halls. He has released eight

CDs, including **Evening Angels.**

Kurt has lived in Utah for most of

his life and finds inspiration at the

top of Mount Timpanogos and at

other Utah natural wonders.

Chicken Mexicali Provo Style

"While on the road early in my music career, I learned to cook this dish from a 70-year-old grandmother. She has since died, but her recipe lives on. We have Chicken Mexicali at least once every two weeks, and we substitute low-fat or fat-free ingredients without compromising the taste. After all, it's the 90s."

4	skinless, boneless chicken breasts
1	10 ¾-ounce can low-fat cream of mushroom soup
1	10 ¾-ounce can low-fat cream of chicken soup
1	4-ounce can chopped green chiles
1	15-ounce can vegetarian chili
1	8-ounce package fat-free shredded Mozzarella cheese
1	package corn tortillas (12)

☀ Preheat oven to 375°

☀ Put the chicken in a saucepan, and cover generously with water. Boil the chicken until no longer pink. Tear chicken into bite-size pieces and reserve a small amount of the broth. Mix together the mushroom and chicken soups, green chiles, vegetarian chili, and a little broth from the boiled chicken.

☀ Tear the tortillas into bite-size pieces.

☀ Cover the bottom of a 2-quart casserole dish with sauce. Add a layer of tortilla pieces, a layer of chicken and a layer of cheese. Continue layering, beginning with sauce, until you have a layer of sauce on top, and finish with a layer of cheese.

☀ Cover and bake for 30 minutes. Remove cover and bake for 15 more minutes. Serves 4-6.

robbie bosco

As Brigham Young University's offensive football coach, Robbie Bosco paces and shouts orders and encouragement to his players. But it wasn't too long ago that Robbie was on the other side of the sideline. The Roseville, California native is best known for leading BYU to the National Championship in 1984, when he guided the Cougars to a 13-0 record and led the nation in passing. He set ten NCAA records at BYU and was second team All-American quarterback. His record as a two-year starter at BYU was 24-3. Robbie, whose pro career was cut short by an arm injury, decided six years ago to return to his alma mater and Utah to raise his family. Robbie, his wife, Karen Holt, and their four children, Amber, Karissa, Alexis, and Dallin, delight in watching the multicolored balloons at Provo's Freedom Festival each year.

Crescent Meat Pies

Crescent Meat Pies are a clever way to dress-up leftover meat.

2	cans crescent rolls (8 rolls per can)
2	cups cooked meat: chicken, tuna, turkey, or roast beef
1	8-ounce package cream cheese, at room temperature
1	small onion, chopped
4	tablespoons hard butter, chopped into small pieces
6	ounces mushrooms, washed and sliced thin salt and pepper, to taste
4	tablespoons butter or margarine, melted
1	package (2 cups) soda crackers, crushed salt and pepper, to taste

☀ Preheat oven to 350°.

☀ Fold each crescent roll into a rectangle, and place between 2 sheets of plastic wrap. Roll the crescent roll into a 3- or 4-inch square. Repeat.

☀ In a mixing bowl, mix together the meat, cream cheese, onion, butter bits, mushrooms, and salt and pepper and combine well.

☀ Place a flattened crescent roll on a flat surface, spoon a dollop of the meat mixture onto one edge of the dough, and roll up. Repeat.

☀ Dip each pie into the melted butter, and roll in the soda crackers.

☀ Place the rolls on an ungreased cookie sheet, seam side down, and bake for 20-25 minutes. Serves 8.

john bower

While he studied economics at Middlebury College, John Bower learned the economics of movement from Nordic skiing. His ability to extract the longest, fastest glide for a sustainable distance carried John to first place at the 1968 Holmenkollen Ski Festival, one of the most prestigious races in the world of cross-country skiing. He also earned a spot on the 1964 and 1968 U.S. Olympic teams. A chance to work for the U.S. Ski Team in the 1980s landed John in Park City, where today he is Ski Jump Complex director at the Utah Winter Sports Park. John, his wife, Bonnie, and their two teen-age children, enjoy Utah's snow bowls and the dramatic tranquillity of Lake Powell.

Monster Cookies

Don't panic when you read the ingredient list. There really isn't any flour in this recipe and the oatmeal quantity is correct.

1	cup butter, at room temperature
2	cups (packed) brown sugar
2	cups granulated sugar
4	teaspoons baking soda
2	tablespoons vanilla extract
3	cups peanut butter
6	eggs, beaten
1	16-ounce package M&Ms
1	16-ounce package chocolate chips
9	cups quick-cooking rolled oats

☀ Preheat oven to 350°.

☀ Cream the butter and both the sugars together in a very large mixing bowl. Add soda, vanilla, peanut butter and beaten eggs, and mix well. Mix in M&Ms, chocolate chips, and oatmeal.

☀ Drop the batter by rounded tablespoons, 2 inches apart, onto an ungreased cookie sheet.

☀ Bake 10 minutes. Cookies should be soft. They become hockey pucks if cooked too long. Makes 6 dozen cookies.

bryce canyon lodge

Bryce Canyon National Park is a world of color and a spectacle of soaring spires and steeples. It is a place to feel the touch of light and earth on the soul. The Bryce Canyon Lodge was built by the Union Pacific Railroad in the 1920s, along with the Grand Canyon Lodge. A National Historic Landmark, the lodge is made of stone and timbers and with its curved roof and shed dormers is reminiscent of a grand Northern European hunting lodge. Architect Gilbert Stanley Underwood, who also designed the Ahwahnee Lodge in Yosemite, took full advantage of the fabulous vistas of nearby Bryce Canyon. The massive wooden trusses, wall-to-wall windows, and gourmet food served in the dining room make eating there an experience not soon forgotten. A stay at the Bryce Canyon Lodge is a step back to a decade of relaxed elegance.

Anasazi Pork Kabobs

Anasazi Pork Kabobs is the signature recipe of the Bryce Canyon Lodge.

4	pounds boneless pork loin, cut into 1-inch pieces

Marinade:

6	tablespoons olive oil
1	cup plus 2 tablespoons Sauterne cooking wine
1	tablespoon granulated sugar
1	garlic clove, minced
1	bay leaf
1	teaspoon whole peppercorns
1	teaspoon cumin
1	teaspoon chili powder
¼	cup thinly sliced onion

Anasazi Sauce:

1	tablespoon margarine
2	tablespoons minced onions
½	teaspoon minced garlic
¾	cup chicken stock
1	cup crushed tomatillos
2	tablespoons minced fresh cilantro
2	tablespoons sweet red bell pepper, diced ½ x ½-inch
½	teaspoon ground cumin
1	tablespoon lemon juice
1	tablespoon corn starch
1	tablespoon cold water

☀ To prepare the marinade: Combine all of the marinade ingredients, and stir. Refrigerate until needed.

☀ Place the cubed pork in a large bowl, pour the marinade over, and stir well to coat each piece of meat. Refrigerate for 24 hours.

☀ To prepare the Anasazi Sauce: Melt the margarine in a saucepan over medium heat. Add the onions and garlic and cook until onions are translucent. Add the chicken stock, tomatillos, cilantro, sweet red bell pepper, cumin, and lemon juice, and bring to a boil. Reduce heat, and simmer on low for 10 minutes. In a glass, combine the

24

corn starch and cold water and mix into a smooth paste. Add the cornstarch to the sauce, stirring until sauce thickens. Keep warm.

☀ Prepare the coals for grilling.

☀ Thread the pork pieces on skewers until you have 8 skewers. Cook the kabobs on the charcoal grill for 4-5 minutes per side, and serve with the sauce. Serves 8.

bruce bugbee

Professor Bruce Bugbee has been involved since 1981 in NASA-supported research on growing food on a lunar colony. In his lab at the Utah State University, wheat is grown in water under high-pressure sodium lamps that produce a light 100 times brighter than a reading light. The result is a hydroponic garden that produces ten times more wheat than a typical wheat field. While it will be quite a while before people grow food on the moon, what Bruce has learned about the factors that affect crop productivity has helped farmers increase yields here on Earth. A fitness buff, Bruce participates every year in the Tour of Two States bicycling fest. Nearly sixty bicyclists pedal a 135-mile loop, beginning in Logan, passing by Bear Lake in Idaho, and returning to Bruce's house, where every one is treated to dinner.

Space Bread

"I got interested in baking bread as a college student. I lived with other students in a cabin near the University of Minnesota in Duluth. We had only a wood-fired stove. On Sunday afternoons during the cold winter months (September to May in Duluth!), we'd invite friends over and bake bread. The wood had to be cut and split into small pieces to control the oven temperature. The stove had three dampers to further control temperature and heat distribution. We constantly tinkered to get perfect loaves of bread.

Now, my wife and I have busy schedules and an automatic bread maker. Temperature is controlled in the bread maker, so I experiment with the ingredients. Baking bread is a chemistry and biology (yeast) experiment in the home laboratory.

Experimenting is more fun when you understand what the ingredients do and how variations can alter the final result. **Yeast** consumes the honey or sugar and produces carbon dioxide gas in respiration, which makes bread rise. Five milliliters (1 teaspoon) of yeast is usually adequate, except when the bread maker is in turbo or quick mode. In turbo mode, the rising time is much less and the yeast doesn't have time to multiply and make enough CO_2 to rise the bread. Too much yeast, more than 20 milliliters, can give the bread a yeast flavor. High protein wheat **flour** is the best for bread because it has the most gluten, the component that binds the bread together and traps the gas that makes the bread rise. You can buy gluten flour and add 30 to 60 milliliters (1-2 tablespoons) of it to other flours to make them rise. **Salt** is for flavoring only. Increasing the salt slows down the yeast metabolism and reduces bread volume. **Milk powder** helps to make a brown crust. Without milk the crust is a very light color. Yeast cannot use the lactose (milk sugar) for its metabolism so the milk is just to add nutrients and darken the crust. Liquid milk and powdered milk give the same result. **Honey** is food for the yeast. Sugar can be substituted but it makes no difference in the bread flavor because the sweetener is consumed by the yeast. I like to use honey produced by the local bee keepers. **Oil** helps to lubricate the strands of gluten, and thus helps the bread to rise. Butter could be used but unsaturated oils keep cholesterol levels down. **Water** increases the bread volume, but too much water causes an excessively moist bread. Have fun experimenting."

10	milliliters yeast, or 2 teaspoons
750	milliliters flour, or 3 cups
5	milliliters salt, or 1 teaspoon
60	milliliters powdered milk, or 2 tablespoons

30	milliliters honey, or 1 tablespoon
30	milliliters oil, or 1 tablespoon
375	milliliters water, or 1.5 cups

Add the dry ingredients (yeast, flour, salt, and powdered milk) to the bread maker. Mix the wet ingredients (honey, oil, and water) together in a beaker. Put the beaker in a microwave with a temperature probe and set the microwave to turn off when the temperature of the liquid gets to 50°C (120°F). This is the optimum temperature for yeast activity. (Lacking a temperature probe, make sure the liquid mixture is warm.) When the liquid is at 50°C, pour it into the bread maker and push Start.

Court of Patriarchs

butch
cassidy
the sequel

Butch Cassidy grew up in the mid-1800s in Circleville, just west of Canyonlands National Park. Later, after a bank robbery or holding up a stagecoach, the outlaw and his boys rode into Canyonlands, where Butch knew every box canyon and ambush point. Few lawmen risked following them into the mazes. Today's Butch Cassidy rides some of the same trails, but instead of hiding from federal marshals, he's looking for new thrills on his mountain bike. Butch the Sequel is more likely a corporate raider armed with a cell phone and fax machine. These inventions have made it possible for people to take their livelihoods to the most remote areas. And that mobility has created a new populace, melding traditional Western cultures— Mormon, ranching, farming, and mining—with influences from around the nation and the world.

Rattlesnake and Rawhide Stew

In the early 1890s, when Butch Cassidy and his Wild Bunch weren't alluding posses in the box canyons of southern Utah, they were riding the sagebrush in search of grub, which more often than not was tougher than rawhide. Today's Butch might prospect for yuppie grub like stuffed olives and sun-dried tomatoes at Trolley Square. His saddle bags may even carry the latest kitchen gadgets, like a set of Calphalon. And, once Butch the Sequel has rustled all of his ingredients together, he'd return to his secret hideout, belly up to the kitchen counter, and cook up a mess of this stew, which is finer than rawhide, no matter which century you live.

2-3	pounds boneless lamb shoulder, cut into 1½-inch pieces

Marinade:

4	tablespoons olive oil
1½	cups white wine
6	garlic cloves, minced
¾	cup stuffed green olives, chopped
5	fresh chiles, cored, seeded, and minced, or more to taste
3	bay leaves
1	tablespoon oregano
1	small red onion, sliced

Stew:

1	tablespoon olive oil
2	tablespoons all-purpose flour
1	cup fresh orange juice
1½	cups beef stock
2	tablespoons tomato paste
5	carrots, peeled, and sliced on the diagonal into 1-inch lengths
2	cups Roma tomatoes, sliced
½	cup sun-dried tomatoes packed in oil, drained, and diced

☀ To prepare the marinade: Combine all of the marinade ingredients in a large bowl. Add the lamb, cover with plastic wrap, and refrigerate overnight, or at room temperature for 2 hours.

☀ Remove the lamb from the marinade. Reserve the marinade. Pat the meat dry.

28

❋ To prepare the stew: In a Dutch oven, heat the olive oil over medium heat, and brown the lamb. Once the lamb is browned, sprinkle with the flour. Stirring frequently, cook long enough to brown the flour, about 2 minutes.

❋ Add the reserved marinade to the Dutch oven, along with the fresh orange juice, beef stock, tomato paste, and carrots. Cover and simmer for 1 hour.

❋ Remove cover, add the Roma tomatoes, and simmer for an additional 15 minutes.

❋ Add the sun-dried tomatoes, and simmer for 10 minutes longer. Serve immediately. Serves 6-8.

Temples and Towers of the Virgin

ingrid butts

Ingrid Butts moved to Utah eight years ago so that she could devote herself to full-time training for the 1988 Olympics. A virtual blizzard on cross-country skis, Ingrid competed in the 1988, 1992, and 1994 Winter Olympic Games. She has dominated racing in the United States for nearly two decades and she has been one of this nation's strongest finisher's in international competitions. Ingrid, a consummate athlete on skis, a bike, or the tennis court, thinks of Utah's wide-open spaces and varied landscape as one huge playground.

My Friendly Poppy Seed Muffins

There is no better way to start a Utah ski day than with light, nutritious muffins. Don't beat the batter too much or the muffins will turn out chewy and tough.

1½	cups whole-wheat flour
1½	cups all-purpose flour
1½	teaspoons baking powder
¾	cup granulated sugar
2	eggs
1	egg white
2	teaspoons almond extract
1½	cups skim milk
3-4	tablespoons apple sauce
2	tablespoons poppy seeds

* Preheat oven to 350°. Lightly grease muffin tin(s).

* In a mixing bowl, combine the whole-wheat flour, all-purpose flour, baking powder, and sugar, and mix well.

* In another bowl, whisk the eggs, egg white, almond extract, skim milk, apple sauce, and poppy seeds together.

* Add the wet ingredients to the dry ingredients, and stir until moistened only.

* Pour the batter into the prepared muffin tins, and bake for 20-25 minutes. Makes 12 muffins.

joe cannon

30

In 1987, when Joe Cannon began asking his Utah friends for financial help to save an idled steel mill, many thought he was crazy. But the then-top-level official with the Environmental Protection Agency didn't give up and within sixty days he and his brother, Christopher, had secured bank financing for the estimated tens of millions of dollars needed to purchase the Geneva Steel Mill. The risk Joe took has translated into thousands of jobs for Utah's and an untold worth to the community. But for Joe, who is now Geneva's CEO and chair, that risk was taken, in part, out of a sense of gratitude. His wife, Janeal, was a secretary at Geneva Works while he was at Brigham Young University in Provo and he credits the mill (and Janeal) for putting him through law school.

Mustard Crumb Chicken Breasts

3	tablespoons grainy mustard, divided
2	teaspoons Dijon mustard
½	cup plain bread crumbs
½	teaspoon salt
	freshly ground pepper
4	large chicken breasts, boned and skinned
1-2	tablespoons olive oil
1	tablespoon butter
2	cups mushrooms, thickly sliced
3	scallions, thinly sliced
½	cup dry white wine
½	cup chicken broth
½	cup heavy cream
	lemon juice

☀ Preheat oven to 375°.

☀ In a small bowl, mix together 2 tablespoons grainy mustard with the Dijon mustard.

☀ In a separate bowl, combine the bread crumbs, salt, and freshly ground pepper.

☀ Wash and dry the chicken breasts. Brush the mustard mixture over each chicken breast, and coat evenly with the bread crumb mixture. Place in a single layer on a plate, cover lightly with plastic wrap, and refrigerate for 30 minutes. Heat the olive oil and butter in a sauté pan over medium heat. Add the chicken in a single layer and sauté, turning once, until browned, about 4 minutes. Transfer the chicken breasts to a baking sheet. Bake the chicken until cooked through and no longer pink, about 15 minutes.

☀ Meanwhile, to the sauté pan, add the mushrooms and all but 1 tablespoon of the scallions, and sauté over medium heat, until limp, about 3 minutes. Pour in the wine and chicken broth and simmer, scraping loose bits from the bottom of the pan, until reduced by half. Stir in heavy cream, and simmer until slightly thickened. Stir in the remaining 1 tablespoon grainy mustard. Increase heat to high, and boil until thick, about 3-4 minutes. Add a few drops of lemon juice, and adjust seasonings.

☀ Transfer chicken to a serving platter. Pour sauce over chicken, sprinkle with remaining scallions, and serve immediately. Serves 4.

canyonlands national park

For eons, the Green and Colorado rivers and their tributaries have carved the sedimentary rock of southeast Utah's Canyonlands National Park, creating some of the most dramatic scenery anywhere. There are wide open skies, mazes of canyons, pictographs left by prehistoric peoples, colorful rock spires, roiling rapids and some of the wildest backcountry in the United States. It is a land of extremes where flash floods, drought, blazing summers, and frigid winds have molded the land and discouraged all but the hardy. Anasazi, Fremont, Ute, and Navajo Indians left stone tools and rock art. Explorers, cowboys, and uranium prospectors followed. Stewart Udall, secretary of the Interior under President Kennedy, and Bates Wilson, superintendent of Arches National Monument, worked to create the park, which was established in 1964.

Dutch Oven Vegetarian Enchiladas

Dutch oven cooking has been used in Canyon Country for over one hundred years. When the cowboys were grazing cattle in the Canyonlands area in the early 1900s, they cooked their food in Dutch ovens. Beans and sour dough biscuits were the main staples. Kent Frost, a writer and an avid explorer of Canyon Country during his youth, operated tours over Elephant Hill in the 1950s. Using traditional outdoor cooking techniques, he prepared Dutch oven meals for his clients. When recently asked for some of his recipes, he said, "Oh, I don't have any recipes! I just threw in a little of this and a little of that. Everyone was so hungry that they enjoyed it." Bates Wilson, father of Canyonlands National Park, used to entertain in the Dutch oven tradition, also. He cooked stews, roasts, beans, and biscuits, but there are no recipes of his to be found. Pretty much the same is told, "a little of this and a little of that."

In the spirit of the cowboys and early residents of Canyon Country, today's employees of the Canyonlands National Park carry on this culinary tradition at their seasonal training campouts by cooking in Dutch ovens owned by Bates Wilson.

3	15-ounce cans red enchilada sauce
2	dozen corn tortillas
1	15-ounce can black olives, drained and chopped
3	4-ounce cans green chiles, chopped
2	15-ounce cans black beans, drained
½	pound fresh mushrooms, sliced
1	large yellow onion, chopped
1	pound Cheddar cheese, grated
2	cups chopped fresh cilantro

Note: This recipe will fill two 12-inch Dutch ovens. You may substitute 5 cups of cooked chicken (skinned, boned, and cut into 1-inch pieces) for the black beans and mushrooms. If making chicken enchiladas, substitute green enchilada sauce for red.

☀ Fire up the coals (about 2 dozen) so they are light gray when you are ready to cook the enchiladas.

☀ Pour enough enchilada sauce into the bottoms of the Dutch ovens to coat evenly. Layer 4 corn tortillas over the enchilada sauce. Place a layer of black olives, green chilies, black beans, mushrooms, and onion on the tortillas. Sprinkle some grated cheese and chopped cilantro over the vegetables. Cover with enchilada sauce.

32

☀ Layer another 4 tortillas over the cheese and cilantro, and continue layering in this manner until the vegetables are gone. Do not layer the enchiladas within 3 inches of the top. The final layer should be tortillas topped by enchilada sauce and grated cheese. Fit the lid tightly on the Dutch oven.

☀ Place the Dutch oven on a bed of 12 hot coals, and carefully place another 12 coals on the lid. Cook 45 minutes to 1 hour. The enchiladas should be bubbling. Remove from the coals, and let sit for 15 minutes before serving. Serves 12.

Red Cliffs

bruce christensen

Barney, Big Bird, MacNeil, and Lehrer were all under his skillful leadership. For ten years, Bruce Christensen was president and chief executive officer of the nation's television network, the Public Broadcasting System. But two years ago, Bruce decided to leave Washington, D.C., and return to his native Utah. He and his wife, Barbara, have renewed many valued friendships at Brigham Young University, where Bruce formerly managed public radio and television stations. He is now the dean of the College of Fine Arts and Communications. Bruce says he "loves tennis, bicycling, and reading, but most of all, I love grandchildren."

Quick French Bread

Making bread need not fill up an entire day. This recipe can be prepared in less than 2 hours, start to finish.

2	tablespoons active yeast, or 2 packages
2½	cups warm water
3	tablespoons granulated sugar
1	tablespoon salt
6	cups all-purpose flour
⅓	cup oil
1	egg, beaten
	sesame seeds

☀ In a small bowl, dissolve the yeast in the warm water, and stir in the sugar. Set the mixture aside until the yeast begins to foam, about 7 minutes.

☀ Combine the all-purpose flour and salt together in a large mixing bowl. Add the yeast mixture and oil. Stir by hand until the mixture holds together and is well mixed. Knead lightly. Cover the bowl loosely with a clean kitchen towel, and let rise in a warm place for 1 hour.

☀ Preheat oven to 400°. Grease a cookie sheet.

☀ Turn the dough out on a lightly floured surface, and form into two long ovals in the traditional French bread shape.

☀ Place the loaves on the prepared cookie sheet. Brush loaves with beaten egg, and sprinkle with sesame seeds. Place the cookie sheet in a warm place, and let the loaves rise again until doubled in size, about 25-30 minutes.

☀ Bake for 20 minutes or until the crust is golden brown. Makes 2 loaves.

When Cori & Merlynn aren't singing for audiences from Nashville to Nephi, Cori Connors is tending her four children, four cats and one dog at home in Farmington, while Assistant Principal Merlynn Schofield is maintaining discipline at Morgan Elementary School in Kaysville. Or, they're doing what comes naturally... shopping at the nearby mall. Together for nine years and counting, the partnership has mounted a steady string of successes. They sang for President Bush, won first place in the Louisville Folk, Blues and Children's Song contests three years in a row, wrote songs recorded by Linda Ronstadt and Chris Le Doux, and generally made people happy with their country and folk songs.

Wasatch Front Pumpkin Roll

Pumpkin Roll:

3	eggs
⅔	cup canned pumpkin
1	cup granulated sugar
¾	cup flour
1	teaspoon baking soda
1	teaspoon cinnamon
	powdered sugar

Filling:

8	ounces cream cheese
2	tablespoons butter, at room temperature
1	cup powdered sugar
1	teaspoon vanilla extract
	chopped nuts, as many as you'd like

☀ Preheat oven to 375°. Line a 15½x10½-inch jelly-roll pan with waxed paper.

☀ To prepare the pumpkin roll: In a mixing bowl, add all of the pumpkin roll ingredients, except the powdered sugar, and beat together well. Spread the batter in the prepared pan, and bake until the top is golden brown, about 12-15 minutes. Cool on a wire rack for 5 minutes.

☀ Spread a clean towel on a flat surface, and sprinkle it lightly with powdered sugar. Invert the cake onto the towel and remove the waxed paper.

☀ To prepare the filling: Beat together all of the filling ingredients, except the chopped nuts.

☀ Spread the filling onto the cake within 1 inch of the edges, and sprinkle the chopped nuts over the filling. Roll the cake up, starting with the short end, until you have a long, thin roll. Arrange it seam-side down on a platter and dust the pumpkin roll with powdered sugar. Serves 12.

stephen r. covey

With five million copies sold, **The Seven Habits of Highly Effective People** *has effectively placed Stephen R. Covey among the world's top management gurus. Stephen has taught leadership principles and management skills for more than twenty-five years to leaders in business, government, and education and founded the Covey Leadership Center to further his outreach. His consulting portfolio includes more than half of the Fortune 500 companies. Stephen has lived in Boston, England, Ireland, and Hawaii, but moved back to his home state to raise his family in Provo. When he wants to effectively relax and enjoy his children, he and his wife, Sandra, escape to Sundance and the family cabin.*

Highly Effective Taco Soup

"My wife Sandra makes this soup because it's fast, good, and nutritious."

1	pound ground beef
1	tablespoon oil
1	medium onion, chopped
1	package mild taco seasoning mix
1	16-ounce can cut corn, drained
1	16-ounce can kidney beans, drained and rinsed
1	28-ounce can stewed tomatoes
1	8-ounce can tomato sauce
	grated cheese
	sour cream
	tortilla chips

☀ In a large sauté pan, brown the ground beef. Drain.

☀ In a separate sauté pan, heat the oil over medium, and cook the onion until limp.

☀ Add the onion to the ground beef, and stir in taco seasonings, corn, kidney beans, stewed tomatoes, and tomato sauce. Simmer 20-30 minutes.

☀ Top with grated cheese, sour cream, and tortilla chips. Serves 6.

herwig demschar

The U.S. Ski Team scored a major victory in 1994, when Herwig Demschar was persuaded to move to Park City and to take the position of Head Women's Alpine Coach. Herwig postponed his plans to take one year off from the pressures of producing champion skiers after nine years of coaching the Austrian national ski team. Since joining the U.S. Ski Team, he has guided the efforts of mature skiers like Picabo Street and Hilary Lindh in world championships and he is developing a string of younger skiers toward greatness. Herwig, his Australian wife, Michelle, and their two sons, Dominic and Daniel, spend half the year in Park City and the other half in Austria.

Puttanesca Arrives in Park City Via Austria

Like the U.S. Womens Ski Team, this traditional pasta dish can hold its own in any country, and is loved all over the world.

1	pound dried pasta, such as capellini or spaghetti
¹/₃	cup plus 1 tablespoon extra-virgin olive oil
6	anchovy fillets, chopped
½	teaspoon chopped garlic
3	cups canned whole, peeled tomatoes, coarsely chopped, with the juice
2	teaspoons fresh oregano, coarsely chopped (or ½ teaspoon dried oregano)
2	tablespoons capers
8-10	black olives, pitted and chopped
	salt and pepper, to taste

☀ Place all but 1 tablespoon of the olive oil in a large saucepan. Add the anchovies. Saute over low heat, stirring with a wooden spoon, until the anchovies dissolve.

☀ Add the garlic and cook for about 15 seconds. Do not brown the garlic.

☀ Raise the heat, and add the tomatoes with a pinch of salt. Simmer the tomatoes until they reduce, about 30-40 minutes. Remove from heat, and set aside.

☀ Meanwhile, bring a large pot of water to a boil. Add the pasta, and return to a boil. Cook until al dente. Drain.

☀ When the pasta is half cooked, return the tomato sauce to the stove. Add the oregano, capers, and olives, and heat through.

☀ Transfer the pasta noodles to a warmed pasta bowl. Toss pasta with the remaining 1 tablespoon olive oil, sauce, and salt and pepper, to taste. Serve immediately. Serves 4.

David's Nacho Casserole

David and Susan Beers submit this recipe on behalf of the Dinosaur Nature Association. Susan is the operations manager for the association. David is described as upholsterer, river guide, kayaker, petroglyph replica maker, fisherman, dirt bike rider, and Vernal, Utah native.

2	pounds ground beef
2	garlic cloves, minced
1½	cups chopped onion
8	ounces cream cheese
1	8-ounce can tomato sauce
¾-1	cup salsa
1	4-ounce can diced green chiles
1	4-ounce can jalapeños, optional
	salt and pepper, to taste
⅓	cup sliced black olives, divided
8	ounces tortilla chips
3	cups grated Monterey Jack cheese
¼	cup chopped green onions
	sour cream, jalapeños, salsa, and tomatoes for garnish

☀ Preheat oven to 375°. Grease a large Dutch oven.

☀ In a large skillet, brown the ground beef.

☀ Add the garlic and onion, and sauté until onions are almost translucent, about 4 minutes. Drain.

☀ Reduce heat, and stir in the cream cheese, tomato sauce, salsa, green chiles, jalapeños, and half the olives. Heat through, and season with salt and pepper.

☀ Line the bottom of the greased Dutch oven with ⅔ of the tortilla chips. Spread the meat mixture over the chips, and top with the remaining chips. Sprinkle the grated cheese, green onions, and remaining olives over the top. Let stand for 45 minutes.

☀ Bake uncovered until cheese is melted, about 30 minutes. Serve with sour cream, more jalapeños, more salsa, and chopped tomatoes on the side. Serves 12.

jane edwards

For the past decade, Jane Edwards has made a huge difference in the lives of countless women and families in Utah. As executive director of Salt Lake City's YWCA, she has offered compassion and concern to the many people with whom she has crossed paths. She has helped women who are escaping violent relationships, low-income women struggling for independence, and pregnant teens, among others.

Jane has seen it all, but she continues as though each day is her first on the job, still enthusiastic about making things better for people. Jane copes with a stressful occupation by seeking solace in Utah's great outdoors. She says she relaxes "where there is greenery, sunshine, and a flat rock on which to recline."

Mardi Gras Carrot Cake

Cake:

1¼	cups oil
2	cups granulated sugar
2	eggs
2	cups grated carrots
1	8-ounce can crushed pineapple, do not drain
3	teaspoons vanilla extract
3	cups all-purpose flour
1	teaspoon salt
1	teaspoon baking soda
3	teaspoons cinnamon
1	cup chopped nuts

Frosting:

1	stick (½ cup) margarine
8	ounces cream cheese, at room temperature
1	teaspoon vanilla extract
1	pound (2 cups) powdered sugar

☀ Preheat the oven to 350°. Grease and flour a 13x9-inch pan.

☀ To prepare the cake: In a mixing bowl, cream together the oil, sugar, and eggs. Add the carrots, pineapple, pineapple juice, and vanilla.

☀ In a separate large mixing bowl, sift together the dry ingredients. Add the carrot mixture, and beat well. Fold in the chopped nuts.

☀ Bake the cake for 60 minutes, or until a toothpick inserted in the center comes out clean. Cool for at least 10 minutes in the pan. Then, invert and remove the cake from the pan. Transfer the cake to a wire rack to finish cooling.

☀ Meanwhile, to prepare the frosting: In a mixing bowl, cream together the margarine, cream cheese, and vanilla. Gradually beat in the powdered sugar. Spread on the cooled cake. Serves 12.

lavell edwards

Coach LaVell Edwards is a dearly loved institution at Brigham Young University. It's no wonder. Since 1972, he has led BYU's football team with integrity, intelligence, and humanity. LaVell has coached more years, won more games, and had a better winning percentage than any other coach in Cougar history. He has been recognized as one of the great minds in the coaching profession and received many awards. LaVell met his wife-to-be, Patti Covey, at Utah State University before entering the Army in 1952. Both Patti and LaVell have continued their academic studies: LaVell obtained a master's and doctorate degree; Patti completed her degree in 1994. The couple lives in Provo and has three married children and twelve grandchildren.

Coach Edwards' Chicken and Artichoke Soup

39

Patti Edwards frequently cooks this soup for her husband, Coach Edwards. It's his favorite.

2	large chicken breasts, skinned and boned
1	medium onion, chopped
1	10¾-ounce can cream of celery soup
1	10¾-ounce can cream of chicken soup
2½	cups chicken stock
1	8-ounce jar unseasoned artichoke hearts, finely chopped
¼-½	pounds jalapeño cheese or other hot Mexican cheese, or a milder cheese, grated
¼	cup half-and-half

* In a soup pot, simmer the chicken breasts and onion in enough water to cover until the chicken is no longer pink. Drain. Chop the chicken into small pieces. Set chicken and onion aside.

* In a large soup pot, combine the cream of celery soup, cream of chicken soup, and chicken stock, and bring to a boil. Reduce heat, add cheese and artichoke hearts and cook until the cheese has melted, stirring constantly. Add the chicken, onion, and half-and-half and heat through. Serves 8.

alan engen

Alan Engen plays an important role in preserving the history of skiing in Utah. He is chairman and president of the Alf Engen Ski Museum Foundation (named after his father); chairman and president of the Alta Historical Society; and a member of the advisory board for the University of Utah Marriott Library Ski Archives Program. He is also part of that history. Alan is a former junior, senior, and masters ski champion in Nordic and alpine disciplines. He was inducted into the Utah Sports Hall of Fame in 1991; is listed among the "Legends of Skiing" in Utah; and was a member of the U.S. Ski Team. A native of Salt Lake City, Alan is currently the director of the Alta ski school.

Alta Pumpkin Bread

"Pumpkin bread has been a traditional Christmas treat for our relatives and friends since the early 1970s."

3	cups granulated sugar
4	eggs
2	cups pumpkin puree
⅔	cup water
1	cup vegetable oil
3½	cups all-purpose flour
1	teaspoon cinnamon
1	teaspoon nutmeg
½	teaspoon salt
2	teaspoons baking soda
½	teaspoon baking powder
1	cup raisins

☀ Preheat oven to 350°. Butter and flour two 9x5x3-inch loaf pans.

☀ Beat the sugar and eggs together in a mixing bowl. Add the pumpkin puree, water, and vegetable oil, and mix well.

☀ In a separate mixing bowl, mix together the flour, cinnamon, nutmeg, salt, soda, and baking powder.

☀ Gradually add the dry ingredients to the wet ingredients, and stir until just blended. Fold in the raisins.

☀ Fill the prepared loaf pans half-full, and bake for 1 hour.

☀ Remove bread from the oven, and cool slightly before removing bread from the pans. Do not let the bread cool entirely in the pan, or the bread will stick to the pan. Makes 2 loaves.

alf engen

Alf Engen was named "Skier of the Century" but perhaps he should have been called "Skier of the Millennium." Alf won the national title in all skiing disciplines—jumping, cross-country, downhill, and slalom—not once, but twice. He was a world ski jumping record-setter, once breaking world records twice in one day. He has pioneered the establishment of thirty major ski areas throughout the United States. Over a quarter million people have learned skiing through the free ski program that Alf started at Alta. Alf and Evelyn Engen have been married for more than fifty-eight years.

Alf's Light-as-Air Angel Pie

"This is a long-time family treat baked for special occasions such as birthdays. In the 1940s, a family friend gave the recipe to my wife Evelyn, who then added her own improvisations, making this the heavenly dessert it is."

Meringue Pie Shell:

4	egg whites
1	cup granulated sugar
½	teaspoon cream of tartar
½	teaspoon vanilla extract

Lemon Filling:

3	egg yolks
½	cup granulated sugar
4	tablespoons lemon juice
2	tablespoons grated lemon rind
1	pint heavy or whipping cream
½	teaspoon vanilla extract
1	tablespoon granulated sugar
	shredded coconut

☀ Preheat oven to 275°.

☀ To prepare the meringue pie shell: In a mixing bowl, whip the egg whites until foamy. Add the cream or tartar, and continue beating until stiff. Gradually beat in the sugar until stiff peaks form and the meringue is glossy. Gently fold in the vanilla extract, and spread in a buttered 9-inch pie pan. Bake for 60 minutes until delicately browned and crusty. Cool.

☀ To prepare the lemon filling: Beat the eggs yolks until thick and lemon colored. Gradually beat in the sugar, lemon juice, and lemon rind. Transfer the filling mixture to a double boiler, and cook over medium heat, stirring constantly, until thick, about 5-8 minutes.

☀ Whip the cream, slowly adding the sugar and vanilla, until stiff.

☀ Spread half of the whipped cream over the crust, then spread the cooled lemon filling. Top the pie with the remaining whipped cream Sprinkle shredded coconut over the whipped cream. Refrigerate until chilled, up to 24 hours.

stein eriksen

Stein Eriksen appears to be a modern-day incarnation of a Norse god. With striking blue eyes and abundant hair, he rules the ski slopes with seemingly boundless strength and grace. Born in Norway to skiing royalty (his father was a ski champion and his mother an expert skier), Stein began competing when he was seven years old. At the 1952 Winter Olympics, Stein won a gold medal in the grand slalom and a silver in the slalom. As director of skiing at Deer Valley, Eriksen's vision has been decidedly instrumental in the resort's success and he has the unique distinction of having the Stein Eriksen Lodge named after him. He, his wife, Francoise, and their four children live at Deer Valley.

Faar I Kaal

"Every family in Norway knows this recipe. The English translation is Lamb in Cabbage. When the lambs were slaughtered in the fall, my mother always made a batch of this stew on Sundays, and we could smell the rich aromas around the house all day. I think it's even better by Monday or Tuesday. When selecting the meat for the stew, be sure to include several different cuts of lamb-ribs, chops, shank, and regular stew meat. The flavor from the bones makes the stew special. Everyone loves Faar I Kaal. I think you will find it nothing but perfect."

1	large head green or red cabbage
4-5	pounds of lamb, various cuts (see above)
	salt and freshly-ground pepper, to taste

☀ Note: This stew cooks all day.

☀ Slice the cabbage into 2-inch square pieces, and set aside. Cut the meat into 1½- to 2-inch chunks, leaving the bone attached.

☀ In a 6-quart pot, put a layer of cabbage on the bottom and spread evenly. Layer a portion of the lamb on top of the cabbage. Sprinkle salt and freshly ground pepper over the meat. Continue layering the cabbage, meat, salt and pepper until the ingredients are gone.

☀ Pour 1 cup of water over the meat and cabbage combination. You shouldn't need to add more water, as cabbage provides a lot of liquid.

☀ Place the pot on a burner, and bring the lamb and cabbage to a boil. Stir. Cover and reduce the temperature to low. The stew needs to simmer at least 6-7 hours. Stir often and check to see if you need to add more water.

☀ If you want to make the stew thicker, you may add a bit of flour at the end. Remove the bones from the stew.

☀ Serve the Faar I Kaal over boiled red potatoes topped with fresh parsley. Serves 8.

Lewis "Lewie" Field knows as well as anyone how to hang on to a buckin' bronc, the equivalent of riding a corralled tornado. Born and raised in Utah, Lewie attended Weber State University in Ogden on a rodeo scholarship. In 1980, he turned professional and during his pro career participated in eleven National Finals Rodeo competitions, a real achievement in itself since only the world's top fifteen cowboys are entered. Twice, Lewie was the World Rodeo Champion in bareback riding, and, three times, he was named All Around World Champion Cowboy. Though retired from the pro circuit in 1991, Lewie is still part of the rodeo realm. At his Diamond G Rodeos ranch in Elk Ridge, Lewie and his wife, Veronica, raise calves and broncs for rodeos all over the country. He says living in Utah, with its four seasons, friendly people, and abundance of hunting and fishing, suits him just fine.

Lewie's Honey Ginger Chicken

3	pounds chicken, drumsticks or thighs, or a combination
⅓	cup all-purpose flour
¾	teaspoon salt
½	teaspoon ground ginger
¼	teaspoon black pepper
3	tablespoons shortening
3	tablespoons butter
⅓	cup honey
⅓	cup chili sauce
½	teaspoon ground ginger

☀ Preheat oven to 425°.

☀ Wash and pat dry the chicken.

☀ In a plastic bag, combine the flour, salt, ground ginger, and black pepper. Add the drumsticks and thighs to the plastic bag, one piece at a time, and coat the pieces by shaking the bag.

☀ In a small saucepan, melt the shortening and butter. Coat the bottom of a 13x9-inch pan with the melted mixture.

☀ Place the chicken pieces, skin-side down, in the pan, and bake, uncovered, for 30 minutes.

☀ Meanwhile, mix the honey, chili sauce, and ground ginger together in a small bowl.

☀ Remove the chicken from the pan, and discard the fat. Line the pan with aluminum foil. Return the chicken to the pan, skin-side up. Pour the honey-ginger mixture over the chicken and bake for another 15 minutes. Serve immediately, or refrigerate and serve later chilled. Serves 6.

debbi fields

At the age of twenty, Debbi Fields cooked up the idea for Mrs. Fields Cookies and started the business from scratch. With utmost confidence in her product, she convinced a bank to finance a chocolate chip cookie bake shop. Nineteen years later, there are more than 600 company-owned and franchised Mrs. Fields Cookies shops in the United States and six other countries with more than 5,000 employees. Debbi serves as chairman of the board for the $100 million business. Debbi also contributes her time and business acumen to philanthropic causes, including the Mrs. Fields Children's Health Foundation, which she founded; and Second Harvest, a non-profit organization dedicated to feeding the hungry. Debbi and her husband, Randi, moved to Park City fourteen years ago to raise their five daughters in a wholesome, family environment.

Debbi's Passion for Pasta

"After I went to Italy last year, I discovered my love for pasta. As a result, I probably eat this pasta dish four times a week. It's low in fat, full of vegetables, and tasty."

1	pound penne pasta
¼	cup extra-virgin olive oil
2	cups broccoli florets
¼	cup sliced leeks
8	garlic cloves, coarsely chopped
½	teaspoon red pepper flakes (optional)
1	cup sliced mushrooms
½	cup dry white wine
¼	cup sun-dried tomatoes, coarsely chopped
½	cup fresh basil, finely chopped
2	medium tomatoes, coarsely chopped
½	cup Asiago cheese, grated
	salt and pepper, to taste

☀ Bring a large pot of water to boil. Add the penne, and cook until the pasta is al dente, about 10-12 minutes.

☀ Meanwhile, in a large sauté pan, heat olive oil over high heat. Add the broccoli florets, leeks, and garlic, and reduce heat to medium-high. Cook until broccoli slightly softens and garlic turns golden, about 3-4 minutes.

☀ Add the optional red pepper flakes, mushrooms, and wine. Continue to cook, stirring often, until the mushrooms soften and the wine reduces by half, about 4-5 minutes.

☀ When the pasta has finished cooking, drain, and add to the sauté pan. Mix well. Stir in sun-dried tomatoes, basil, fresh tomatoes, and salt and pepper, and cook for another 2 minutes.

☀ Transfer pasta to a warm serving dish, toss with Asiago cheese. Serve immediately with additional grated Asiago on the side. Serves 4.

holly
flanders

This is one stone who will gather no moss. Holly Flanders is on a roll. The former two-time Olympian is in her ninth year as director of skiing at major Utah resorts and currently runs the show (as director of skiing and mountain biking) at Wolf Mountain Resort. Holly, who has three World Cup downhill wins, understands racing and her commentary for ESPN and Turner Sports is always fresh and insightful. At the 1992 Winter Olympics in Albertville, France, Holly hosted radio programs from around the United States. More recently, Holly starred in **Let's Go Skiing***, an instructional video released by ABC Video. She also conducts women's ski workshops, race camps, and private clinics at Wolf Mountain. But at home are what she considers her greatest accomplishments, her two children, Beth Anne and Alex, along with husband Todd Schlopy.*

Almost Healthy Chocolate Chip Cookies

"I love chocolate chip cookies, but I don't like the fat and sugar. I've come up with this recipe so that I can eat chocolate chip cookies with a little less guilt. They're not exactly a normal, gooey cookie, but to me they represent a great compromise."

1	stick margarine or butter, at room temperature
½	cup applesauce
¾	cup brown sugar
½	cup granulated sugar
2	eggs, beaten
1	teaspoon vanilla extract
2	cups whole wheat flour
2	cups rolled oats
1	teaspoon baking soda
1	teaspoon salt
1	cup chopped walnuts, or raw sunflower seeds
3	cups chocolate chips

☀ Preheat oven to 375°. Lightly grease baking sheets.

☀ In a large mixing bowl, cream together the margarine, applesauce, brown sugar, and granulated sugar. Add the beaten eggs and vanilla extract.

☀ In a mixing bowl, stir together the whole wheat flour, oats, baking soda, and salt.

☀ Gradually add the dry ingredients to the wet ingredients, and stir until smooth. Stir in the nuts and chocolate chips.

☀ Drop the batter by rounded tablespoons, 2 inches apart, onto the prepared baking sheets. Bake for 10 minutes.

☀ Cool the cookies on a wire rack. Makes 8 dozen.

bob frankenberg

Novell is a high-tech miracle. Started in 1980, the Provo-based maker of computer peripherals nearly failed in 1983. Today, Novell is the number-one maker of networking software, with a seventy-five percent market share. With the acquisition of Word Perfect and Quattro Pro, Novell has become the fourth largest independent software maker in the world. In 1994, Bob Frankenberg took the company's helm. Prior to joining Novell, Bob was vice president of Hewlett-Packard Company. Bob, who colleagues describe as affable and unassuming, has taken to living in Utah, hook, line, and sinker. He is an ardent angler, whose private passions are, first, his wife, Linda, and second, fishing. A native of Chippewa Falls, Wisconsin, Bob holds a bachelor's degree in computer engineering from California's San Jose University.

Novell's Nouveau Scaloppine al Marsala

Veal Scaloppine smothered in Marsala wine and mushrooms is rich and perfect for an entrée in any season.

4	boneless veal cutlets (about 2 pounds)
	flour, salt and pepper
6	tablespoons butter, divided
5	tablespoons olive oil, divided
½	cup Marsala wine
½	cup chicken stock
2	garlic cloves, minced
1	pound mushrooms, cleaned and quartered
1	medium yellow onion, sliced thick
3	tablespoons fresh parsley, chopped
	parsley sprigs (optional)

☀ Lay the veal between two pieces of waxed paper, and flatten each piece with a meat pounder until ¼-inch thick. Sprinkle cutlets lightly on both sides with flour, salt and pepper.

☀ In a heavy skillet, melt 2 tablespoons butter over medium-high heat and add 3 tablespoons olive oil. Add the veal and sauté until lightly browned, about 2-3 minutes per side. Do not overcook. Veal requires very little cooking. Remove the veal from the skillet and set aside.

☀ Pour the fat from the skillet. Add the Marsala and the chicken stock, and bring to a boil. Boil for 1-2 minutes, scraping any meat bits left in the skillet into the mixture. Add 2 tablespoons butter, reduce heat to low and simmer for 7-10 minutes.

☀ Meanwhile, in a separate skillet, melt 2 tablespoons butter over medium heat and add 2 tablespoons olive oil. Add minced garlic and sauté for 1 minute. Stir in mushrooms, onion, and parsley. Cover, and cook until the mushrooms are slightly tender. Pour off excess liquid.

☀ Return the veal to the skillet with the Marsala, and just heat through. Top with the mushroom mixture and serve immediately. You may garnish with parsley, if desired. Serves 4.

Where's the best place to eat in Salt Lake City? There are eight correct answers to this question: Baci Trattoria, a most delectable kiss of Italy with an extensive menu of traditional favorites; Club Baci, the pulse of the city with wood-burning ovens and a Northern Italian menu; Pierpont Cantina, a festive setting for the cuisine of Mexico; New Yorker, American cuisine at Gastronomy's premier establishment; China Star, a contemporary Chinese menu in a sparkling setting; and the Market Street Oyster Bar, the Market Street Broiler and the Market Street Grill, all offering the freshest fish and seafood from around the world. The art of eating is captured in Gastronomy's eight Salt Lake City restaurants.

A Salt Lake Garden's Vegetable Stew

1½	pounds fresh tomatoes
4	tablespoons canola oil, divided
2	cups small pearl onions, peeled, or 2 medium white onions, sliced into 1-inch dice
3	garlic cloves, minced
2	tablespoons cumin
1	whole jalapeño
1	tablespoon fresh minced oregano, or 1½ teaspoon dried
1½	teaspoons salt
1	teaspoon granulated sugar

Any combination of 6 or 7 of the following:

1	cup snapped yellow beans, cut into 1-inch pieces
1	cup snapped string beans, cut into 1-inch pieces
1	cup yellow squash, cut into 1-inch pieces
1	cup green squash, cut into 1-inch pieces
1	cup turnip, cut into 1-inch pieces
2	cups carrots, cut into 1-inch pieces
1	large red bell pepper, cut into 1-inch pieces
1	large green bell pepper, cut into 1-inch pieces
	corn kernels cut from 3 ears of corn
1	ear of corn, cut into 1-inch pieces
¼	cup parsley, chopped
¼	cup cilantro, chopped

☀ Set oven to broil. Coat the tomatoes with about 2 tablespoons of the canola oil, and broil for 12-15 minutes, until shriveled and blackened. Place tomatoes and juices in food processor or blender, and puree. Set aside.

☀ In a small stock pot, heat 2 tablespoons canola oil over medium heat. Saute the onions and garlic until brown. Add the pureed tomatoes and 2 cups water. Add the cumin, jalapeño, oregano, and salt and simmer. Add the combination of vegetables you have chosen, except the corn kernels and corn. Cover and simmer for 15 minutes. Add the corn and sugar and cook, covered, for 5-10 minutes longer. Remove from heat, and serve immediately. Top with chopped parsley and cilantro. Serves 6-8.

jim gordon

Professor Jim Gordon sometimes dresses up in costumes to get his point across to law students at Brigham Young University. In an attempt to teach students to write precisely and clearly, his Elvis lectures on getting the fat out of legal writing and his football player stresses the importance of tackling verbosity. Jim is well known for his sense of humor in class and in numerous publications, including his book **Law School: A Survivor's Guide.** *Jim says those in the legal profession tend to take themselves too seriously. So his teachings are a reminder to students and attorneys that sometimes humor and humility are needed when handling legal matters. Jim, his wife, Nadine, and there nine children live in Orem, where, Jim jokes, a large family is required by zoning laws.*

Fresh Summer Pasta Sauce

The beauty of this timeless Italian pasta sauce lies in its simplicity. Use only sweet, plump sun-ripened tomatoes and fresh herbs from the garden or a farmer's market.

1	garlic clove, halved
2	pounds fresh tomatoes, cored, seeded, and diced
⅓	cup olive oil
2	garlic cloves, minced
¼	cup chopped fresh parsley
¼	cup slivered fresh basil leaves
¼	teaspoon salt

☀ Rub the inside of a non-reactive bowl with the halved garlic cloves.

☀ Put the fresh diced tomatoes in the bowl. Add the olive oil, minced garlic, fresh parsley, fresh basil, and salt. Mix the ingredients with a spoon.

☀ Cover the bowl with plastic wrap, and let it sit for 2 hours at room temperature. Then, chill before serving.

☀ Serve the chilled sauce over your favorite hot pasta noodles. Serves 4.

gorgeous

Gorgeous moved to Utah ten years ago, looking forward, like many who immigrate, to improvements in her lifestyle. Gorgeous has benefited from many of the wonderful things Utah has to offer. In 1990, physicians from the University of Utah Medical Center removed cataracts from her eyes. When she could see all of her loving and admiring visitors, Gorgeous became much more energetic and engaging. But the lifestyle change that made the biggest difference was the gift of friendship. In 1993, the Hogle Zoo staff in Salt Lake City carefully introduced N'jina, a ten-month-old kitten, to the 190-pound female primate. Gorgeous gently put the kitten in her favorite bowl and proudly paraded around with the kitten balanced on her head. Today, Gorgeous, who is forty six and the oldest gorilla living in captivity, looks forward to a long life with N'jina.

Gorgeous' 46th Birthday Cake

The Hogle Zoo sends special thanks to Marge Jones and the animal care staff for creating this wonderful birthday cake for Gorgeous.

1 ½	cups monkey chow
½	cup all-purpose flour
¼	teaspoon baking powder
¾	teaspoon baking soda
1	egg, beaten
⅔	cup unsweetened orange juice
1	20-ounce can crushed unsweetened pineapple
1	carrot, finely grated
½	cup raisins
2	tablespoons non-fat, non-cholesterol margarine
4	Bosc pears, peeled and cubed
½	teaspoon cinnamon

☀ Preheat oven to 425°.

☀ In a large bowl, combine all ingredients. Mix by hand until thoroughly blended.

☀ Pour mixture into two round cake pans.

☀ Bake for 40 minutes.

☀ Remove from oven, and cool for 10 minutes. Ice with non-fat dairy whipping cream, and garnish with cherry tomatoes. Makes 1 cake for 1 gorilla.

flip harmon

As chairman of the Days of '47 Rodeo and president of the Days of '47 Festival, Flip Harmon heads up one of the world's biggest rodeos and Utah's most popular celebration. The Days of '47 commemorates the pioneers' arrival on July 24, 1847 and includes parades, fireworks, and the PRCA Rodeo at the Delta Center in Salt Lake City. The seventh of ten children, Flip was born in Magna and, except for a stint on a Navy destroyer during World War II, he has lived in this small community at the base of the Oquirrah Mountains all of his life. He enjoys Utah's seasonal climate, especially the fall when he saddles his favorite horse for long rides to hunt in his beloved mountains.

Days of '47 Oatmeal Cookies

1	cup raisins
1	cup water
¾	cup shortening
1½	cups granulated sugar
2	eggs, beaten
1	teaspoon vanilla extract
2½	cups all-purpose flour
½	teaspoon baking powder
1	teaspoon baking soda
1	teaspoon salt
1	teaspoon cinnamon
½	teaspoon ground cloves
2	cups rolled oats
½	cup walnuts, chopped

☀ In a saucepan over low heat, simmer the raisins and water until raisins are plump, about 20-30 minutes. Drain raisin liquid into measuring cup. Add or drain enough water to make ½ cup.

☀ Preheat oven to 400°.

☀ In a large mixing bowl, cream together the shortening and sugar. Beat in the eggs and vanilla. Add the raisin liquid.

☀ In a separate mixing bowl, sift together the flour, baking powder, baking soda, salt, cinnamon, and ground cloves.

☀ Gradually add the dry ingredients to the wet ingredients. Add the rolled oats, raisins, and walnuts, and stir in.

☀ Drop the dough by rounded teaspoons onto an ungreased baking sheet, about 2 inches apart. Bake 8-10 minutes, until lightly browned. Transfer cookies to a wire rack to cool. Makes 6-7 dozen.

trent harris

Trent Harris' first film, **The Orkly Kid**, *featured an introverted teen-age cross dresser. Then in 1991, came* **Rubin and Ed**, *a cult comedy about two guys trying to bury a dead cat in the desert. In 1995, the Salt Lake City resident unleashed* **Plan 10 from Outer Space** *at the Sundance Film Festival and it has since developed a national cult following. In one scene from the science-fiction fantasy, Trent's Straffordshire terrier travels to the moon with a rocket strapped to his back. Trent says he is "way outside the mainstream and happy to be there."*

Oyster-Chile-Garlic Stuff

- spaghetti noodles
- butter
- garlic
- hot dried red chile peppers
- canned oysters
- fresh parsley
- lime juice
- olive oil

I like this recipe because you can make it in ten minutes, and it only costs four bucks. First, boil up some spaghetti noodles. While that's going on, melt some butter in a different pan, and throw in as much chopped garlic as you can stand. Be sure you peel the garlic first, or people will think you are a complete dope. While the chunks of garlic are sautéing, cut up a couple of hot dried red chile peppers. Whatever you do, don't stick your finger in your eye after cutting up those chiles. It burns like hell, and could cause permanent blindness. Put the chiles in with the garlic and butter, and stir them around. Now, open up a can or two of oysters and drain off all that weird juice. I recommend flushing the oyster juice down the toilet, so that it won't stink up your entire apartment. By now your spaghetti noodles are done, so pour them into a strainer. While the noodles are draining, throw the oysters in with the garlic and chiles. **Don't cook them, just heat them up.** Squirt a little bit of lime juice on the oyster-chile-garlic stuff. Put some spaghetti in a bowl and add a little olive oil. Put the oyster-chile-garlic stuff on top of the spaghetti, add a little salt, sprinkle some cut up fresh parsley over the whole thing, and you're ready to eat. I hope you enjoy the stuff.

john hart

As artistic director for Ballet West, John Hart has carefully nurtured young talent and developed many superb dancers who have retained their own distinctive qualities. John says, "If you encourage artists to believe in themselves, you'll find that they will make the extra effort and go beyond what they believe is possible." John modestly understates his own career, but it is a shining example for his dancers. He was one of England's most distinguished dancers and ballet directors, and performed those functions for the Royal Ballet of England before bringing his talents to this country. As a dancer, he performed all the leading roles and was a partner to such illustrious ballerinas as Margot Fonteyn and Moira Shearer. Ballet West's future will be anything but staid with John at the helm. He says, "We must preserve the classic ballets, but we have to take risks and build toward the future."

Traditional English Christmas Pudding

1	pound suet, finely chopped
1	cup bread crumbs
1½	cups all-purpose flour
1	whole nutmeg, grated
½	teaspoon cinnamon
½	teaspoon ground cloves
1	teaspoon salt
2	cups brown sugar, packed
4	cups seedless raisins
2	cups dried currants
½	cup candied orange peel
8	eggs, slightly beaten
½	cup cold milk
½	cup shelled almonds, blanched and chopped fine
½	cup brandy or rum, to flambé the pudding

* In a large mixing bowl, mix together the suet, bread crumbs, all-purpose flour, nutmeg, cinnamon, ground cloves, salt, and brown sugar. Add raisins, currants, candied orange peel, eggs, and milk. Mix well.

* Spoon the pudding mixture into the center of a clean, wet, and well-floured 20-inch square cotton cloth. Beginning with one corner of the cloth, gather folds together about the pudding and tie a string around the cloth, leaving extra room for swelling.

* Bring a large pot of water to a boil, and place the pudding in a steamer. Steam for 6 hours. Replace the water as needed.

* Remove the pudding from the steamer, and hang for 1 week in a cool, dry place.

* Just before serving, steam the pudding again for an additional 3 hours. Turn the pudding into a serving bowl, and dot with the blanched almonds. Douse with warmed brandy or rum and ignite with a long kitchen match. The flame will die out quickly. Garnish the pudding with a sprig of holly, and serve with whipped cream, custard, brandy or rum butter. Note: The holly is for looks only—it's poisonous. Serves 12.

dee holladay

In 1960, Dee Holladay took his first river trip. In the course of three days, the Yampa River captivated the young man's soul. Within six years, he had turned running rivers and being in the wilderness—what he loved most—into Holiday River Expeditions. At a time when "environmental responsibility" was not in vogue, Dee was at the forefront, advocating smaller tour group sizes, controlled access to fragile areas, and mandatory "pack it out" rules. Today, Holiday River Expeditions is a leader in wilderness ethics and its trips on Utah, Colorado and Idaho rivers are conducted with a special appreciation of the natural forces that formed the scenery so enjoyed by visitors. While running the business side demands that Dee spend considerable time in the Salt Lake City office, he always saves time for himself on the river. After thirty years, that's what he loves most.

Dutch Oven River Potatoes

10	large potatoes
1	large onion, sliced
1	can beer
1	pint sour cream
½	teaspoon black pepper
1	garlic clove, minced
	salt to taste
1	pound Cheddar cheese, grated
	sprinkle of paprika
	parsley for garnish

✳ Cut the potatoes in half lengthwise. Cut each half into thin slices. Place the potatoes and onion in a Dutch oven, and pour the beer over them. Add enough water to cover. Bring to boil, and simmer until potatoes are tender. Drain.

✳ Add the sour cream, black pepper, garlic, and salt to the Dutch oven and blend gently. Place spoonfuls of grated Cheddar cheese into pockets formed in the potatoes. Smooth mixture and finish with a layer of cheese on top. Sprinkle paprika and parsley over the cheese for garnish.

✳ Cover the Dutch oven and set next to the fire to melt the cheese. Serve sitting next to your favorite river. Serves 10.

pam houston

54

For author Pam Houston, living in Park City was ideal. For nine years in the late 1980s and early 1990s, Pam settled into the easy-going rhythm of the small resort town. Up with the sun, Pam wrote until she says she got bored with herself. When the snow fell, she wrote less and skied more, occasionally hiking to the top of Scott's Bowl, the highest accessible point at Park City, to look out at the Wasatch front, Mt. Timpanogos, and acres of untracked snow. Those sights and the friendships Pam made in the community are woven by bits and pieces into **Cowboys Are My Weakness**, her best-selling collection of short stories. Pam is currently working on her first full length novel.

Pam's Ceviche

"Okay, Okay—Here it is:"

1	pound fresh Chilean sea bass (or other firm, white fish)
1	large red onion, chopped
1	bunch fresh cilantro, stems removed, and chopped
4	garlic cloves, minced
6	lemons
3	limes
1	tablespoon red wine vinegar
¼	teaspoon Habanero pepper sauce, or to taste
	salt and pepper, to taste

☀ Cut the fish into ½-inch pieces.

☀ Put the red onion, cilantro, and garlic into a bowl. Squeeze the lemons and limes, and add the juice to the bowl. Stir in the red wine vinegar, Habanero pepper sauce, and salt and pepper.

☀ Marinate the fish in the onion-cilantro mixture for 15-20 minutes.

☀ Chill before serving in a pretty bowl. Serve with crackers, tortilla chips, or crostini. Serves 6.

lou hudson

Lou Hudson's life is punctuated with superlatives. Lou was the first Minnesota college basketball player to become an All-American. After graduating, he was drafted by the St. Louis Hawks in the first round. The 6-foot-5 forward scored an average of 20.2 points per game during his thirteen-year career with the St. Louis Hawks, the Atlanta Hawks, and the L.A. Lakers. He retired when he was thirty-five years old, and moved to Park City to marry his former college sweetheart, Mardi Smith. He was voted Rotarian "Citizen of the Year" in 1992, in part, because of the recreation camps he runs for Summit County youths. In 1993, Lou became Utah's first black City Council member when he won the Park City election. The North Carolina native says that Utah is the best, "No humidity, no bugs, great mountains."

All Star Vegetable Bake

4	cups finely chopped fresh spinach
2	cups finely chopped Swiss chard
4	cups finely chopped leeks
4	eggs
2	tablespoons all-purpose flour
1	teaspoon salt
1	teaspoon freshly ground black pepper
3	tablespoons butter, melted
¼	cup grated Parmesan cheese
¼	cup grated Fontina cheese
1	tablespoon butter
	fresh parsley, chopped, for garnish

☀ Preheat the oven to 350°. Butter or grease a 3-quart casserole dish.

☀ In a large bowl, mix together the chopped spinach, Swiss chard, and leeks.

☀ In a separate mixing bowl, combine the eggs, flour, salt, pepper, and melted butter, and mix well.

☀ Add the egg mixture to the vegetables. Stir in the grated cheeses.

☀ Pour the vegetable mixture into the prepared casserole dish. Dot the top with the remaining 1 tablespoon butter.

☀ Bake until the center is firm, about 35-40 minutes.

☀ Garnish with fresh parsley, and serve. Serves 6.

jamie kurlander-peters

For Jamie Kurlander-Peters it seems like eons since she was ranked among the world's top fifteen in giant slalom and downhill, although it was just seventeen years ago that Jamie placed seventh in the downhill World Cup races. But then life has moved at a fast clip for Jamie who has three children: Max, seven; Tosh, five; and Tali, four months. Jamie and her husband, Dean, own and run a ski shop, Park City Sport. Life is never dull for the Peters. When they first opened, Maria Shriver's skis were temporarily misplaced by the shop and Dean had to tell the Terminator the news. Dean shook like a leaf while the rest of the staff hid behind the counter. Luckily, they were quickly found. Jamie says, "Now we write everyone's name on their skis."

Cocoa Pink Cuplets

"These cupcakes look a bit pink from the chocolate after they are cooked. I hope you enjoy them as much as my family does."

2	cups flour, or a little more for high-altitude
1	tablespoon cocoa
1	teaspoon salt
1¼	cups granulated sugar
¾	cup shortening or margarine
2	eggs, beaten
2	teaspoons vanilla extract
1	teaspoon baking soda
1	cup cold water
1	cup semi-sweet chocolate chips
½	cup chopped walnuts

☀ Preheat oven to 375°. Line two 12-cup muffin tins with fluted paper baking cups.

☀ In a mixing bowl, combine the flour, cocoa, and salt. Set aside.

☀ In a large mixing bowl, cream together the sugar and shortening or margarine. Blend in the beaten eggs and vanilla.

☀ In a cup or glass, combine the baking soda and water, and stir well. To the creamed mixture, add the dry ingredients alternating with the water and soda mixture, beginning and ending with the dry ingredients. Blend thoroughly after each addition.

☀ Spoon the batter into the prepared pans, filling each cup about half full. Sprinkle the semi-sweet chocolate chips and walnuts over the cupcake batter. Bake for 20 minutes, or until a toothpick inserted in the center of a cake comes out clean. Cool for a moment before turning them out onto a rack to cool thoroughly. Makes 2 dozen cuplets.

frank layden

*In 1983, Utah newcomer Frank Layden transformed the uninspired Utah Jazz basketball team into the 1983-84 Midwest Division champion with his strategic genius. He was named the 1984 NBA Coach of the Year. In 1988, Frank decided he wanted to spend more time with his wife, Barbara. But Utahns didn't want to see him retire, so they found a way to keep him. As Jazz president, Frank continues to contribute to the success of the team. In their leisure time, the Laydens enjoy and support the performing arts, especially the theater, and recently starred in Salt Lake Acting Company's **Love Letters**. A Brooklyn-born Irish Catholic, Frank says that he has found a home in Utah's capital.*

Slam-Dunk Chicken

This is a good recipe for people on-the-go, and the presentation is festive and colorful.

4	large chicken breasts, cut into bite-sized pieces

Marinade:

1	bottle Wishbone dressing
	or
6	tablespoons olive oil
3	tablespoons red wine vinegar
½	teaspoon dried basil
¼	teaspoon dried marjoram
¼	teaspoon dried oregano
⅛	teaspoon dried rosemary, crushed
½	teaspoon salt
½	teaspoon black pepper
1	large yellow onion, coarsely chopped
2	red, yellow or green bell peppers, cored, seeded, and coarsely chopped
½	pound fresh mushrooms, chopped in half
1	garlic clove, minced

✺ To prepare marinade: Use Wishbone dressing, or in large mixing bowl, combine olive oil, red wine vinegar, basil, marjoram, oregano, rosemary, salt and pepper. Mix well.

✺ Add chicken, onion, peppers, mushrooms, and garlic to marinade and refrigerate for at least 3 hours or overnight.

✺ Preheat oven to 350°. Transfer chicken, vegetables and marinade to a roasting pan and bake for 45 minutes. Serve over rice. Serves 4.

Alta Mayor Bill Levitt says that it is impossible to make remuneration for having the opportunity to live in Alta and raise his family there. But this esteemed public servant has certainly made an extraordinary effort. In fact, he has served on nearly as many volunteer committees, councils, advisory boards, and associations as the number of years he has lived in Utah—forty-one. It all started in 1959, when Bill visited Alta and fell in love with the place. He sold everything he owned in New York, moved to Utah, and eventually was able to buy the Alta Lodge, which he still owns and manages.

High Alta-Tude Chocolate Soufflé

"Many years ago I ate at a small restaurant back East that served only filet mignon and chocolate soufflé. I asked them for the soufflé recipe, but we had a problem getting it to work at Alta's high altitude, 8,600 feet. After much trial and error, we got it right and started serving chocolate soufflé at the Alta Lodge. At that time, it was the only soufflé served in the entire state of Utah. It's still the most popular item on our menu."

2	tablespoons butter
½	tablespoon flour
1	cup milk, scalded
4	eggs, separated
½	cup granulated sugar, divided
3	squares unsweetened chocolate
1	teaspoon vanilla extract
	a pinch of salt
	brandied whipped cream

☀ Preheat oven to 350°.

☀ In a double boiler, melt the butter, and then add the flour. Whisk until smooth. Mix in the scalded milk, and turn the heat to low.

☀ In a small bowl, beat the egg yolks until creamy yellow, and add ¼ cup sugar, mixing well. Add the egg yolks to the milk mixture. Raise the heat to medium, and, stirring often, cook until thick and the mixture pulls away from the sides of the pan.

☀ In a separate double boiler, melt the chocolate squares. Add ¼ cup sugar and a pinch of salt, and mix well. Add this chocolate mixture to the milk custard mixture, stir in the vanilla extract, and blend together. Cover the double boiler completely with wax paper, and set aside until it reaches room temperature.

☀ While waiting for the chocolate mixture to come to room temperature, beat the egg whites in a mixing bowl until stiff. Once the chocolate mixture has reached room temperature, fold in the egg whites.

☀ Pour the soufflé mixture into 8 individual ramekins. Set the ramekins in a 13x9-inch pan and carefully pour 1-inch water into the pan. Bake for 30 minutes, or until the soufflé is puffed. Serve immediately with brandied whipped cream. Serves 8.

hilary lindh

Hilary Lindh is America's downhill heroine. She won an Olympic silver medal at Albertville, France, in 1992. In 1994, she became the first American woman in a decade to win a World Cup Downhill when she skied fearlessly at Sierra Nevada, Spain. At twenty-five years old, Hilary is just reaching her prime. She is ranked second in the international downhill standings, just behind teammate Picabo Street, and is poised to become the world's premier female skier at the 2002 Winter Olympics. A native of Juneau, Alaska, Hilary has lived and trained in Utah since high school. She lives at Wolf Mountain and studies exercise physiology at the University of Utah.

Mom's Green Spaghetti

"Green Spaghetti was a favorite of mine while I was growing up and remains so today because not only does it taste good, it's really easy to make, even for me."

1	pound spaghetti noodles
1	stick (½ cup) margarine
⅓	cup olive oil
3-6	whole garlic cloves
1	bunch parsley, finely chopped
1	tablespoon dry sweet basil
¾	bunch broccoli, chopped
1	cup grated Parmesan cheese

☀ In a large skillet, melt the margarine. Add the olive oil, garlic, parsley, basil, and broccoli. Cook over low heat for 30 minutes. Discard the garlic cloves.

☀ Meanwhile, bring a large pot of water to a boil. Add the spaghetti, and return to a boil. Cook until al dente, about 10-12 minutes. Drain.

☀ Mix the spaghetti and vegetable sauce together in a large pasta bowl, and top with Parmesan cheese. Serves 4.

lopeman's frontier movie town

Step back into time to the days of the Old West. In every detail, Lopeman's Frontier Movie Town in Kanab resembles life as it was in the 1800s. There's a livery where antique tackle hangs and an anvil marks the toil of generations past.

At one corner, a pioneer's house, constructed of fiberglass to look like sod for the movie **Outlaw Jose Wales**, *reminds many visitors of the hard and dank life of their predecessors. Ray and Marcia Lopeman moved to Utah in 1988 to be closer to their church and to establish the frontier town— a lifelong dream.*

Cowboy Roast Beef

Although a bottom round roast is considered a tougher cut of beef, this method of roasting insures a flavorful and tender roast.

1	5- to 6-pound bottom round roast
4-5	tablespoons Worcestershire sauce
1	tablespoon garlic salt
1	tablespoon onion salt
1	tablespoon seasoning salt
1	package beef soup base
	water

☀ Preheat oven to 325°.

☀ Pierce the roast with a knife about 7 times on each side. The slits should be about 2 inches long, and ½ inch deep.

☀ Wet the entire roast heavily with the Worcestershire sauce.

☀ Mix the garlic salt, onion salt, seasoning salt, and beef soup base together in a bowl. Sprinkle the mixture on both sides of the roast.

☀ Place the roast in an oven roasting bag. Add 2 cups of water to the bottom of the bag. Close the bag and pierce it several times.

☀ Place the bag in a roasting pan, and fill the pan with several inches of water. Bake the roast for 5½ hours. Check the roast often to see if you need to replenish the water in the pan.

☀ Allow the roast to sit for 10 minutes before slicing.

☀ The juices from the roast may be used for au jus or beef stock, and can be diluted with water, if necessary. Serves 10.

elle macpherson

Elle's Shrimp on the Barbé

Elle sends this recipe from her Manhattan restaurant, The Fashion Cafe.

10	large shrimp, peeled, and deveined
4	tablespoons unsalted butter
1	carrot, peeled and cut into julienne
1	yellow squash, cut into julienne
1	zucchini, cut into julienne
⅓	cup white wine
¼	cup chopped fresh cilantro
2	flour tortilla cups, available at specialty stores, warmed
½	cup salsa
¼	cup cilantro paste

☀ In a large sauté pan, melt the butter. Add the shrimp, and julienned vegetables, and sauté for 2 minutes, stirring continually. Remove the shrimp and vegetables from the pan. Keep warm.

☀ Add the white wine and fresh cilantro to the pan, and deglaze for 1 minute.

☀ On two plates, arrange 5 shrimp on the edge of each plate.

☀ In the center of the plate, arrange the julienned vegetables.

☀ Place a flour tortilla cup on top of the vegetables, and fill with salsa.

☀ Drizzle each plate with the cilantro paste, and serve immediately. Serves 2.

Megamodel Elle Macpherson successfully crossed over into the world of film with her debut in the movie **Sirens.** *Just before its Sundance Film Festival premier in Park City, Elle was nervous about facing the critics for the first time. Dressed in a black catsuit and ski sweater, the 6-foot Australian beauty said she felt like a fish out of water. But those jitters were all for not.* **Sirens** *and Elle were praised.*

While Elle decides what she'll do next, she hardly has to worry about spare time between modeling shoots and managing the businesses built on her name. Those interests include a lingerie firm, co-ownership in Manhattan's Fashion Cafe, exercise videos, and an annual calendar.

62

The dream is to build a 1,000 seat auditorium, where students can discover the magic of theater and music, and where Park City residents can revel in the beauty of a Ballet West performance or the Utah Symphony. Behind every dream, every grassroots effort of this magnitude, are the dreammakers, those volunteers whose vision, sacrifice and perseverance enrich their communities for all. As president of the board of the Park City Performing Arts Center, Ann MacQuoid is this kind of citizen. Ann, her husband Mac, and the many other board members and volunteers who have so selflessly given their time and energy to this project, will see their dream to reality.

Rheinischer Sauerbraten

Mac MacQuoid says, "I lived in Austria and Bavaria many years ago, during which time I dreamed of opening a place like the Goldener Hirsch restaurant in Salzburg, owned by Countess Hariett Walderdorff. I finally opened my own Goldener Hirsch Inn in Deer Valley.

Although the Countess is quick to point out that Rheinischer Sauerbraten dish is not Austrian, it is one of Goldener Hirsch's specialties, and one of our personal favorites. It is best with potato pancakes, red cabbage, and chunky applesauce."

Spiced Vinegar Marinade:

6	cups water
2	cups red wine vinegar
2	teaspoons salt
4	large white or yellow onions, diced
2	large carrots, diced
10	peppercorns
4	whole cloves
2	bay leaves
4	juniper berries, or more
4	pounds beef bottom round, in 1 or 2 pieces (do not use prime cut of meat)
	lard or shortening, for browning the meat
1	cup raisins
	salt and pepper, to taste
2	lebkuchen (or gingerbread crumbs)
2	tablespoons apple syrup (or dark corn syrup)
2	cups sour cream

☀ To prepare the marinade: Mix all of the marinade ingredients in a large pot. Bring to a boil, and simmer for 20-25 minutes. Set aside to cool. Drink a glass of Liebfraumilch and enjoy your work.

☀ Place the meat in a deep glass dish, and pour the cooled marinade over it. Cover, and store in the refrigerator for 4-7 days. Turn daily. The longer it sits, the deeper the flavor. This will also give you time to brush up on your German history.

☀ When you are ready to cook, preheat the oven to 350°. Drain the meat, reserving the marinade. Pat the meat dry, and brown it in the lard or shortening in a large Dutch oven. Strain the marinade, removing the vegetables and seasonings. Pour the strained marinade over the browned meat. You may wish to add more water as the sauce tends to reduce more than I like. Cover the Dutch oven.

☀ Bake the meat until tender, basting often, about 2½ hours.

☀ Meanwhile, soak the raisins in warm water for 20 minutes. Drain.

☀ Add the raisins to the Dutch oven about 2 hours into baking the meat.

☀ Transfer the well-cooked meat to a platter. Keep warm. Break for wine.

☀ Skim the fat from the remaining sauce, and season with salt and pepper. Stir in the lebkuchen or gingerbread crumbs to thicken the sauce. Add the syrup, and stir in the sour cream. Warm through.

☀ Slice the sauerbraten and serve with lots of sauce. Serves 12.

Calico Rock

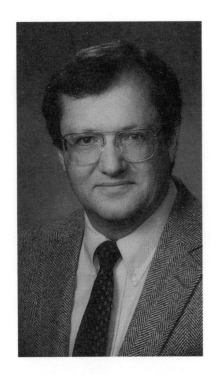

richard madsen

On October 15, 1868, Brigham Young summoned a group of community leaders to meet at Salt Lake City's City Hall. The result was the organization of Zions Cooperative Mercantile Institution, a community-owned merchandising establishment. To this day, hundreds of families whose forefathers subscribed for ownership shares still own stock in ZCMI. While ZCMI pioneers had no idea they were making merchandising history, it has since been established that they founded America's first department store. More than 100 years later, with CEO Richard Madsen in charge, ZCMI has taken a strong stance as Utah's premier retailer with thirteen stores spanning across the state. Richard holds degrees in law, interior design and business. He and his wife, Doralee, have ten children.

Barbecue Flank Steak

Richard Madsen, chairman of ZCMI, was a cook in the Army, where he received the Silver Frying Pan Award. He says he doesn't do much cooking at home because he only learned to cook for crews of 250 or more. However, he is good at the grill, and often fixes this favorite for his family of twelve.

2	flank steaks, about 3 pounds each

Marinade:

¼	cup soy sauce
1	teaspoon ground ginger
¾	cup oil
¼	cup honey
1	garlic clove, minced
1	bunch green onions, finely chopped

 To prepare the marinade: Put the soy sauce, ground ginger, oil, honey, minced garlic, and green onions in a food processor, and spin the blade until the mixture is fairly smooth.

Place the flank steaks in a 13x9-inch glass or non-reactive pan, pour the marinade over, and cover loosely. Marinate the flank steaks overnight in the refrigerator, or for at least 4 hours. If only marinating for 4 hours, allow the steaks to sit at room temperature for the last hour. Turn the steaks often to coat both sides.

Prepare the barbecue for grilling.

Grill the steaks for about 5-8 minutes per side, depending upon the thickness.

Slice the meat thinly on the diagonal and serve on a large platter. Serves 12.

rick majerus

Off court, University of Utah basketball coach Rick Majerus is gregarious and witty. But, Rick, widely recognized as one of the nation's top college coaches, is all business on court. He has high expectations of all his players, especially in the classroom. He repeatedly reminds his young men that education is a privilege and of the immeasurable value of a college education. He engenders tremendous respect from his players, and, in turn, they give him 100 percent. That has translated into a remarkable six-year record. He has steered his young Utes to several Western Athletic Conference titles, three NCAA tournaments, and to the NIT "Final Four." Rick is a native of Sheboygan, Wisconsin.

Fast Break Brownies

2	squares Bakers semi-sweet chocolate
1	cup plus 2 teaspoons shortening
2¼	cups granulated sugar
5	eggs
1	teaspoon salt
2	teaspoons vanilla extract
2	cups all-purpose flour
1	cup chopped nuts

☀ Preheat oven to 350°. Grease and flour an 11x8-inch pan.

☀ In a double boiler, melt the chocolate squares and shortening.

☀ In a large mixing bowl, mix together the sugar, eggs, salt, and vanilla. Gradually stir in the flour.

☀ Add the chocolate mixture to the sugar and egg mixture. Fold in the nuts.

☀ Pour batter into the prepared pan, and bake for 30 minutes. Makes 2 dozen brownies.

j.w. marriott jr.

J. W. Marriott Jr. humbly says he is not as good a businessman as his father. The senior Marriott pioneered the Hot Shoppe restaurant chain. His son, now sixty-three, has turned his inheritance into a $7.4 billion hotel-and-catering empire, one of the world's largest and most successful hotel chains and still seventeen percent family-owned. Born in Washington, D.C., the young Marriott was trained in banking and finance at the University of Utah. He joined his father's company in 1956 and today he is chairman of the board and president of Marriott International, which operates more than 100,000 hotel rooms worldwide. For three successive years, Marriott has won Business Travel News' top hotel chain award. He and his wife, the former Donna Garff, have four children and eleven grandchildren and are active members of The Church of Jesus Christ of Latter-day Saints.

Marriott's Chili Con Carne

Chili Beans:

3	pounds plus 8-ounces dry chili beans
3	tablespoons salt
½	cup margarine
1	cup chopped onion
2	teaspoons Worcestershire sauce
1	tablespoon prepared mustard
6	tablespoons tomato puree
½	teaspoon white pepper
1	cup barbecue sauce

Chili Meat:

7	ounces salt pork, rind removed before weighing
4	pounds plus 11-ounces ground beef
4	garlic cloves, minced
3	tablespoons chili powder
5	teaspoons salt
½	teaspoon cayenne pepper
1½	cups chopped onion
¼	cup chopped celery
1	cup tomato puree
5	tablespoons all-purpose flour
	water

 To prepare the beans: Wash the beans and pick over for stones and bad spots. Soak the beans in 5 quarts of cold water for about 18 hours. Rinse the beans. Place the beans in a very large stock pot and add 5 quarts of water. Add salt and simmer until the beans are just soft. Do not overcook.

Melt the margarine in a skillet and cook the onion until transparent. Add the Worcestershire sauce, prepared mustard, tomato puree, white pepper, and barbecue sauce, and cook just until well mixed. Add the beans to the sauce. Simmer slightly to blend.

To prepare the meat: Slice the salt pork into paper thin slices. Cook the salt pork in a very large skillet over low heat until slightly browned. Remove cracklings and discard. Save fat. Add the ground beef, garlic, chili powder, salt, cayenne pepper, onion, celery, and tomato puree to the skillet, and cook over high heat, stirring frequently, until the ground beef is no longer pink. Add 1 quart plus 1 cup water to the meat mixture, and simmer over low heat until the meat is tender, about 1 hour. Combine the flour with 1 cup water, and add to the meat mixture. Cook until thickened, approximately 4 minutes.

☀ Add the beans to the meat mixture and heat through. Makes 2¼ gallons.

Canyon Paradise

john middendorf

68

John Middendorf has been defying gravity most of his adult life. He is the world's leading practitioner of big wall climbing, a mix of rock climbing and alpine-style mountaineering which requires climbing rock faces more than 2,000 feet tall and, by necessity, spending nights on the vertical plane. He lists fourteen first ascents, including: The Atlantic Ocean Wall, a face of El Capitan; The Kaliyuga, the north-west face of Half Dome; and Abraham in Zion National Park. A tournament-rated chess player, Stanford University engineering graduate, computer wizard, juggler, and tightrope walker, John co-authored **How to Rock Climb: Big Walls** *with John Long, and is the owner of A5 Adventures, a manufacturer of hanging tents, called Portaledges.*

Thai Peanut Sauce

This peanut sauce adds liveliness to your favorite pasta or steamed vegetables. John likes the sauce over spaghetti or linguine noodles.

½	cup peanut butter
1	small onion, grated
1	garlic clove, minced
4	teaspoons soy sauce
3	teaspoons lemon juice
¼	teaspoon honey
¾	cup coconut milk
	ground chili peppers, optional

In a saucepan, combine all ingredients and mix well. Add hot water until the mixture has a creamy consistency. Simmer over low heat, stirring often, until cooked through, about 10 minutes. Serve hot. Makes 2 cups.

moab to monument valley film commission

Thelma and Louise did it. So did Wes Studi in **Geronimo.** *Before them John Wayne rode through the sandstone needles and isolated, inspiring landscapes of Moab and Monument Valley.* **Stagecoach, 2001: A Space Odyssey, Easy Rider,** *and* **Forrest Gump** *are just a few of the other movies filmed there. John Wayne summed up the appeal of this area when he said: "TV you can make on the backlot, but for the big screen, for the real outdoor dramas, you have to do it where God put the West." The Moab to Monument Valley Film Commission has been assisting production companies for more than forty-five years in southeastern Utah and is the oldest continuously operating film commission in the United States.*

Pineapple Matinee Cake

"The film industry is on a fast track, and quick and easy recipes, with plenty of flavor, are savored by the Moab to Monument Valley Film Commission," says Executive Director Bette Stanton.

2	eggs
2	cups granulated sugar
1	20-ounce can (2 cups) crushed pineapple and juice
1	teaspoon vanilla extract
2	cups flour
2	teaspoons baking soda
¼	teaspoon salt
1	cup chopped walnuts (optional)

☀ Preheat oven to 350°. Grease a 13x9-inch pan, and lightly dust with flour.

☀ Beat the eggs and sugar together in a mixing bowl. Add the pineapple chunks and juice, and vanilla and mix well. Mix the flour, soda, and salt together in a bowl and gradually add to the pineapple mixture. Beat until smooth. Fold in the chopped walnuts.

☀ Pour the batter into the prepared pan, and bake for 30 minutes. Cool the cake and frost with your favorite cream cheese frosting.

☀ Fat Clue: For those watching their diet, omit the walnuts and frosting. Serves 12.

In their westward quest across the vast American continent, the pioneering Mormons often broke the prairie's stillness with singing. Upon crossing the rugged Wasatch Mountains on July 24, 1847, their leader, Brigham Young, looked onto the wide valley of the Great Salt Lake and declared it home. Ten years later, the first hymn was performed in the Salt Lake Tabernacle on Temple Square, one of the world's finest auditoriums. The Tabernacle is so acoustically sensitive that a pin dropped at one end can be clearly heard at the other end, 170 feet away. In a proud tradition, choir members are drawn from all walks of life, including contractors, secretaries, physicians, school teachers, and homemakers. All contribute their talents and time without compensation.

Tabernacle Turkey

Merrill L. Wilson, M.D., a former member of the Mormon Tabernacle Choir, submits this recipe on behalf of the group. He sang with the choir for over twenty years. Notice his clever instructions, gleaned from years in the medical profession.

"Frequently, roast turkey is poorly seasoned, and the meat is dry. This method of roasting a turkey insures excellent seasoning and moistness of the meat."

1	10- to 12-pound turkey
	salt and pepper

Sage Dressing:

1	cup butter
1	large onion, finely chopped
1⅓	teaspoons salt
1	tablespoon sage
⅛	teaspoon pepper
2	teaspoons thyme or poultry seasoning
1	large loaf of bread (about 1½ pounds)
1	cup turkey stock, or chicken stock
3	eggs, well beaten

To prepare the sage dressing: Melt the butter in a medium sauté pan, and sauté the onion. Add the salt, sage, pepper, and thyme or poultry seasoning. Break the bread into rather large pieces, and place the bread pieces in a large mixing bowl. Pour the butter mixture over the bread, and mix. Add the turkey stock and beaten eggs. Mix thoroughly.

Wash the turkey thoroughly in cold water. In order to gain access to the meat of the turkey so that proper seasoning can be applied, the skin beginning at the outlet is mobilized and elevated and with blunt dissection with the hand, the fibrous bands of connective tissue are divided over the breast laterally toward the back and behind the thighs and the legs. The only skin that cannot be mobilized well is that directly on the back and on the wings. Salt and pepper are mixed together in a small bowl. The amount varies with the desires of the cook. The salt and pepper mixture is placed in the hand and then rubbed thoroughly under the skin over the breast down toward the back and on all sides of the thighs and legs. The wings and neck are peppered and salted separately onto the skin. The dressing is placed not only in the cavity but inside the skin adjacent to the breast, the back and around the thighs and legs. The turkey is then trussed securely, wrapped thoroughly in heavy aluminum foil, placed on a rack in a large pan and placed in a preheated oven at 400°. The turkey is roasted at 400° for $1\frac{1}{2}$ hours after which the temperature is reduced to 225° and cooked slowly for another 11 hours. The high heat is initially given in order to destroy any pathogenic bacteria that may have been present in the flesh of the turkey or in the dressing. At the conclusion of the roasting time, the meat should literally fall off the bones. Serves 8-10.

Kolob Canyons

david "sparky" mortimer II

What does the future hold for a nine-year-old sportscasting wizard from Alpine, Utah? David "Sparky" Mortimer has already appeared on ESPN II twice, helped out with televised play-by-play for Brigham Young University football games, and interviewed athletes on nearly a dozen radio programs across the nation. David Letterman asked him back after Sparky proved to be an articulate and immensely entertaining guest. He was flown to New York City and honored as the "Future of Sportscasting" by the American Sportscasters Association. But Sparky, the grandson of the publisher of the **Salt Lake City Deseret News,** *is content living in the present. "I'm young," says Sparky, "I like being young."*

Sparky's Sport Brownies

½	cup butter
⅓	cup cocoa powder
1	cup granulated sugar
2	eggs, lightly beaten
1	teaspoon vanilla extract
1¼	cups all-purpose flour
¼	teaspoon baking powder
⅛	teaspoon salt
	powdered sugar

☀ In a saucepan, melt the butter over medium heat. Remove from heat. Stir in the cocoa. Add sugar, eggs, and vanilla, and stir until well blended. In a mixing bowl, blend together the flour, baking powder, and salt. Gradually add the dry ingredients to the wet, and stir well.

☀ Spread the batter into a greased 9x9-inch glass baking dish or a 9-inch glass pie plate. Cover with microwave plastic wrap. Microwave on high for 4 minutes. Uncover, rotate the brownies a quarter—turn, and microwave uncovered for 1-2 minutes longer. Cool. Sprinkle with powdered sugar and serve to your sport fans. Makes 16 brownies.

The National Institute of Fitness is nestled in one of nature's most stunning creations. Located near St. George and with Snow Canyon State Park in its backyard, the spa is surrounded by desert wilderness, red rock canyons, and lava flows. It is here that guests are introduced to the natural beauty of life, fitness, and well-being. Exploring geological wonders with more than 30 different walking trails, finding flavors and satisfaction in eating expertly prepared low-fat and low-sugar meals, and relaxing with a massage or facial are some of the activities that place the Institute among the nation's finest spas. **Shape Magazine** *called NIF "the best outdoor fitness program on earth—located in the most scenic area of any spa."*

Raspberry Cookies

¾	cup whole-wheat flour
½	teaspoon baking powder
¼	teaspoon baking soda
3	tablespoons fructose
1	teaspoon egg replacer or egg substitute
2	tablespoons apple sauce
1	tablespoon raspberry extract
3½	tablespoons fresh raspberries
¼	cup pineapple juice

☀ Preheat oven to 350°. Spray a cookie sheet with a light coating of Pam, or other cooking spray.

☀ In a mixing bowl, combine the whole-wheat flour, baking powder, and baking soda. Add the fructose, egg replacer, apple sauce, raspberry extract, fresh raspberries, and pineapple juice. Mix thoroughly.

☀ Drop the batter by tablespoon onto the baking sheet.

☀ Bake for 8-10 minutes. Makes about 2 dozen cookies.

navajo nation

The Dineh (The People) believe that there are two classes of beings; the Earth People and the Holy People. Centuries ago the Holy People taught the Dineh—the Navajo—how to live the right way and to conduct the daily work of life. They were taught how to live in harmony with Mother Earth, Father Sky, and all the elements found on Earth. The Navajo Nation stretches into three states—New Mexico, Arizona, and Utah—and is larger than the entire state of West Virginia. The Navajo people hold on to their cultural essence, cherishing their language and artistic, spiritual, and culinary heritage.

Authentic Buffalo Stew

Chef Regis T. Tsosie sends this savory stew recipe from the Navajo Nation Inn. He says, "The longer you cook it, the hotter it gets." There are nearly 1,000 varieties of chiles, from fiery hot to sweet and mild. For the faint-of-heart, we suggest using milder Anaheim, Tuscan (pepperoncini), or poblano (ancho) chiles.

5	pounds buffalo stew meat, cut into 1-inch pieces
4	cups Anasazi beans, soaked overnight (adzuki or pinto beans may be substituted)
2	tablespoons vegetable oil
6	ribs celery, sliced into 1-inch lengths
½	pound carrots, peeled, and sliced into 1-inch lengths
1	large onion, chopped
4	cups stock or water
4	cups green chiles, chopped
4	cups sweet corn
2	pounds tomatoes, chopped
2	garlic cloves, minced
1	tablespoon barbecue seasoning
1	tablespoon freshly ground black pepper
1	tablespoon salt

☀ Drain the beans and place them in an 8-quart Dutch oven. Cover with water, and bring to a boil. Reduce heat, and simmer until the beans are soft, about 1½ hours, replenishing water as needed. Drain.

☀ In a large skillet, sauté the buffalo meat in the vegetable oil over medium-high heat until browned. Add the celery, carrots, and onions, and cook over medium heat for 5 minutes.

☀ In a large stock pot, combine the beans with the buffalo mixture. Add the stock or water, green chiles, corn, tomatoes, garlic, barbecue seasoning, black pepper, and salt. Simmer for 30 minutes. You may add cornstarch to thicken stew, if necessary. Serves 12-14.

lisa needham & rich wyman

When Lisa Needham and Rich Wyman moved to Park City five years ago, they brought with them some special talents. Rich, a singer and songwriter, has traveled throughout the country, touring with such artists as Robert Palmer. Recently, Rich linked up with Eddie Van Halen and Andy Johns to produce a recording that has wowed the critics. A list of Lisa's talents is extensive. She is an accomplished screen and television actress who can execute a variety of dialects and faces. She is also a certified personal fitness trainer, a yoga instructor, an illustrator, a jewelry designer, a white water rafter, a gymnast and, if necessary, she can walk across the room on her hands. Rich and Lisa love to take their baby, Ian, on hikes in the great Utah outback.

Lamb-A-Jam

"Late one night some friends came over for a barbecue. After several hours of drinking and eating, someone began banging on a pot. Before we knew it, we had an all-night jam. Hence, the name Lamb-A-Jam."

1	leg of lamb, butterflied (about 5-6 pounds after boning)
	soy sauce
	fresh garlic
	onions
	crushed red cayenne peppers or cayenne pepper

You start with a leg of lamb. Ask your butcher to butter fly it and remove the bone. Place it in a huge bowl and douse with soy sauce. I like it swimming in soy sauce. Crush "muy mucho" amounts of fresh garlic. I mean clove after clove. I mean lots of the stuff. With your bare hands mash the garlic into every nook and cranny of the lamb. Work it baby. Work it. Then cut up some onions. A couple, maybe three. Stuff the onion into the lamb, but not as intensely as the garlic. Last, but not least, stuff the lamb with crushed cayenne peppers. The hottest ones you can get your hands on. Powdered cayenne pepper works well, too. Apply the peppers generously. Cover the bowl with plastic wrap and place in refrigerator overnight.

On the evening of the announced festivities, break out the Weber, or other large charcoal grill. I find the Weber's vast circumference especially suitable. Pile the coals, soak for a minute with fuel, and light. At this time, you must soak a bowl of hickory chips in water. When the coals are good and hot and white and ready, spread 'em out and evenly cover them with the soaked hickory chips. Remove the lamb from the bowl, roll it, and tie it up with butcher's twine. Place your lamb on the grill and let it smoke!!!

Cook until medium rare (50-60 minutes), turning often. Then slice it like a London Broil. Serve it either in a big bowl or on a plate. It will be gone in seconds. It's that good! Serves 6-8.

Next, break out the pots, the pans, the drums, whatever, and bang on into the night. Have fun.

marilyn hanold neilson

As a New York actress, then-Marilyn Hanold was a frequent television face on **Bewitched, The Bob Hope Show, The Carol Burnett Show**, and many others. In the film **Solid Gold Cadillac** the classic beauty played a seductress. Then she met Utah oil baron Rulon Neilson. They married, had children, and Marilyn gracefully switched gears to become his companion and right-hand man. She supervised the renovation and improvement of the Salt Lake Airport Hilton Hotel, of which she was the managing general partner. She was vice president for the Neilson Brothers Energy Company and the Skyline Oil Company, working closely with Rulon in those endeavors. Recently, Marilyn has returned to the stage. She played Lilliane La Fleur, the lead role in the Salt Lake Acting Company's production of **Nine,** and received many accolades for her performance.

Marilyn's Baked Macaroni

1 ½ cups elbow macaroni pasta shells

Cream Sauce:
1   tablespoon butter
1   tablespoon all-purpose flour
2   cups milk
    salt and pepper, to taste
2   cups sharp Cheddar cheese, grated
    bread crumbs
    butter

 Preheat oven to 350°. Butter a 3-quart casserole dish.

 Bring a large pot of water to a boil. Add the macaroni pasta shells, and cook at a rolling boil until al dente, about 7-8 minutes.

 To prepare the cream sauce: In a large saucepan, melt the butter. Add the flour, and whisk over low heat for a few minutes until well-blended, but do not brown. Add the milk, and salt and pepper to taste. Whisk constantly over medium heat until mixture thickens, about 5 minutes.

 Add ⅓ of the macaroni shells to the prepared casserole dish. Then add ⅓ of the grated cheese, and continue alternating layers until the macaroni and grated cheese are gone. Pour the cream sauce over the macaroni. You can add some milk if you think you need more moisture. Sprinkle the top with bread crumbs and dot with butter. You can put the casserole dish in a pan filled with 1 inch of water to keep the pasta moist. I sometimes put a cover on my dish and take it off towards the end to brown. Bake for 30-40 minutes. Serves 4.

merlin olsen

Merlin Olsen, a former member of the Los Angeles Rams' "Fearsome Foursome," was hardly fearsome as FTD's soft-spoken advocate for sending a loved one flowers. In 1975, after fifteen years of remarkable performances on the football field, Merlin became NBC's top NFL analyst and covered five Super Bowls before moving to CBS Sports. The gentle lineman went on to play Jonathan Garvey in the television series **Little House on the Prairie.** *An enthusiastic volunteer, he has raised funds for the Children's Miracle Network, Child Help USA, and the Multiple Sclerosis Society. Merlin was born and raised in Logan, Utah, and after butting heads in Los Angeles for many years, he returned to live in Park City.*

Park City Omelet

This is a hearty and satisfying omelet, a fine beginning to a vigorous day on the slopes or cross-country skiing.

2	tablespoons butter
1	small cooked potato, thinly sliced
¼	cup thinly sliced onion
¼	cup diced cooked bacon
3	tablespoons shredded Cheddar or Monterey Jack cheese
3	eggs
2	tablespoons half-and-half
	salt and freshly ground black pepper
1	tablespoon olive oil

☀ Melt butter in a medium skillet. Add potato and onion, and sauté over medium-high heat until onions are golden and potatoes nearly crisp. Stir in bacon, and sauté for 1 more minute. Remove from heat, stir in cheese, and set aside.

☀ In a small bowl, lightly beat together the eggs, half-and-half, and salt and pepper to taste.

☀ Heat oil in an 8-inch, non-stick omelet pan over medium heat. Add egg mixture, and cook without stirring until the omelet starts to bubble around the edges. Continue cooking until the bottom is set but the top is still slightly wet. Spread the potato mixture over half of the omelet. Fold the other half over the filling, and cook until heated through, about 30 seconds. Slide the omelet onto a plate and serve at once. Serves 1-2.

jeff olson

Jeff Olson says a combination of factors-chasing an old love, a condo acquisition, and SKIING—lured him to Utah. Love's eternal pull not withstanding, skiing may have been the strongest magnet. Jeff was a member of the U.S. and Olympic ski teams from 1985 to 1994. During those years, Jeff was a three-time U.S. National Downhill champion and a Pan American gold medalist in giant slalom. A gregarious, likable guy, Jeff was a U.S. Ski Team captain for four years, and has continued in leadership roles as a spokesperson representing Utah's bid for the Olympics, director of the Corporate Ski Classic (a fund-raising program for the U.S. Ski Team), and a Park City Ski Area ambassador. Jeff has broad interests that span foreign languages (he's fluent in French and German), computers, carpentry, hiking in the wilderness, and volunteering his time for good causes.

Sun-Dried Tomato Pesto

"I married an Italian... Good **hot** pasta. Good **red** wine. Good **passionate** love. This is a fun recipe for Italian Wannabes, like me. You can serve the pesto over your favorite pasta, have some more wine, and enjoy. Grazi!"

3	cups sun-dried tomatoes packed in oil, drained
1 ½	cups extra-virgin olive oil
1	cup grated Parmesan, Romano, or Asiago cheese
½	cup toasted pine nuts
1	cup packed fresh Italian parsley, stems removed
3-5	garlic cloves (depending upon how friendly you are with the partakers of this dish)

☀ To begin this recipe properly, have a glass of wine. I suggest Banfi or Ruffino Chianti, or whatever your budget permits, so long as it's red.

☀ Place all of the above ingredients in a food processor and let fly.

☀ If you don't have a food processor, have a glass of wine, and do it the old-fashioned way. Chop, chop, chop.

☀ And, finally, keep the arts performing, by supporting the performing arts. Makes 6 cups.

jimmy osmond

Jimmy Osmond is that rare mix of talented artist and successful businessman. As the youngest member of the renowned Utah family, The Osmonds, Jimmy received the first of many accolades at age five when he scored the first gold record in his family. A highlight of his singing career was a command performance for the Queen of England. The left side of Jimmy's brain hasn't lagged behind. Before Jimmy turned fifteen, he had developed and overseen the Osmond's merchandising business. An adept businessman, Jimmy has produced and promoted events around the world, including Michael Jackson's record breaking Japan tour and Disney on Ice, and created and developed numerous enterprises, including the Osmond Family Theater in Branson, Missouri.

Cottage Pasta Salad

1	pound linguini

Marinade:

1	garlic clove, minced
1	cup olive oil
½	cup red wine vinegar
¼	teaspoon Worcestershire sauce
½	teaspoon ground pepper
¼	teaspoon salt
1	tablespoon dried oregano
2	tablespoons minced fresh parsley
½	cup pine nuts
2	cups freshly grated Asiago cheese
12	sun-dried tomatoes packed in oil, drained, and diced

☀ Bring a large pot of water to a boil. Add the linguine, return to a boil, and cook until al dente, about 6-8 minutes. Drain. Pour the pasta into a large bowl.

☀ Meanwhile, to prepare the marinade: Combine the garlic, olive oil, red wine vinegar, Worcestershire sauce, ground pepper, salt, oregano, and fresh parsley in a jar. Put the lid on, and shake.

☀ Pour the marinade over the pasta noodles, and toss. Cover, and refrigerate for 8-12 hours.

☀ Place a third of the noodles into a large glass serving bowl. Layer a third of the pine nuts, cheese, and sun-dried tomatoes. Continue in this fashion until all the ingredients are gone. Serve at room temperature. Serves 4-6.

marie osmond

Marie Osmond is Utah's favorite daughter. She was only three years old when she made her show-business debut on **The Andy Williams Show** *with her singing brothers, The Osmonds. At the age of fourteen, she became the youngest person to co-host a weekly television variety series when she and her brother, Donny, starred in the top-rated* **The Donny and Marie Show.** *For many years, Americans have wanted her back. And back she is, starring in the ABC sitcom,* **Maybe This Time,** *with Betty White. With a heart as big as her talent, Marie co-founded the Children's Miracle Network and has helped raise hundreds of millions of dollars for children's hospitals throughout the United States, Canada, and New Zealand. Marie loves spending time with her husband and their four children at their mountainside home in Provo.*

Marie's Killer Cheesecake

"When making the crust, I put the crackers in a large zip-lock bag and let the kids crush them with a can. They love it."

Crust:

1	package (2 cups) graham crackers, crushed
3	tablespoons melted butter
2	tablespoons granulated sugar

Filling:

3	8-ounce packages cream cheese, at room temperature
¾	cup granulated sugar
3	eggs
1	teaspoon vanilla extract

Topping:

1	8-ounce container sour cream
1	teaspoon granulated sugar
1	tablespoon vanilla extract

☀ Preheat oven to 350°.

☀ To prepare the crust: Put the crushed graham crackers in a mixing bowl, and add the sugar and melted butter. Mix until the mixture holds together. Using the back of a spoon, press the mixture into an 8-inch springform cheesecake pan. Bake for 10 minutes, and remove from oven.

☀ Lower the oven temperature to 300°.

☀ To prepare the filling: Combine the softened cream cheese and sugar in a mixing bowl. Add the eggs, one at a time, and mix well. Add the vanilla with the last egg. Spoon the filling into the baked crust, and bake for 1 hour at 300°. Remove the cheesecake from the oven, and let sit for 10 minutes.

☀ To prepare the topping: Mix the sour cream, sugar, and vanilla in a mixing bowl. Top the cheesecake with the sour cream mixture and refrigerate for at least 3 hours. Garnish with strawberries or the fruit of your choice before serving. Serves 8.

arnold palmer

The golf ball Arnold Palmer drove from the top of a 900-foot column in Utah's Monument Valley may have been his loftiest ever. The famous shot is one of many television commercials Arnold has made as America's most famous and well-liked golfer. And the powerful Arnold, the first professional golfer to amass $1 million in tournament earnings, has left more than divots in Utah. He designed the state's number one-ranked Jeremy Golf Course in Park City. Arnold, a Pennsylvania native, loves the crisp, clear air of Utah's links, the world's best environment for a hole-in-one.

Hole-in-One Meat Balls

Meatballs:

1 ½	pounds ground beef
⅔	cup cracker crumbs
½	cup chopped onion
⅔	cup evaporated milk
1	teaspoon seasoned salt
⅓	cup all-purpose flour
3	tablespoons shortening

Sweet-Sour Sauce:

1	14-ounce can pineapple chunks
2	tablespoons cornstarch
½	cup vinegar
½	cup brown sugar
2	tablespoons soy sauce
2	tablespoons lemon juice
1	cup coarsely chopped green pepper
1	tablespoon chopped pimiento

 To prepare the meatballs: Combine the ground beef, cracker crumbs, onion, evaporated milk, and seasoned salt, and mix lightly but thoroughly. Shape mixture into 30 balls. Roll in flour. Heat the shortening in a large skillet, and brown the meatballs in batches. Drain the meatballs on a paper towel, and return all of the cooked meatballs to the skillet.

To prepare the sweet-sour sauce: Drain the pineapple chunks, reserving the syrup. Add the syrup to a measuring cup and add enough water so that the mixture equals 1 cup. In a medium-sized saucepan, blend together the pineapple liquid and cornstarch until smooth. Stir in vinegar, brown sugar, soy sauce, and lemon juice until smooth. Cook over medium until thickened and clear. Add the pineapple chunks, green pepper, and pimiento and mix well. Cover and simmer over low for 15 minutes.

Pour the sauce over the meatballs and simmer, covered, over medium-low heat for 15 minutes. Serves 6.

jan peterson

In 1980, Jan Peterson opened the first Jans Mountain Outfitters store in Park City. Over the years, his attention to detail and expert consumer service have placed his stores at the top of **Snow Country** *magazine's list of Top Ski Shops. Now, Jans Mountain Outfitters is the largest volume locally-owned sporting goods retail business in the Intermountain area with seven outlet locations in Park City. When Jan isn't busy tending to his stores he still finds time to enjoy his favorite sport, fly-fishing. Jan says, "Each hour spent fishing adds a day to your life." You can frequently find him extending his longevity on one of Utah's blue ribbon trout streams.*

Trout Ceviche

1	pound fresh trout, skinned, boned, and cut into bite-size pieces
1	cup fresh lemon juice
1	onion, minced
1	tomato, peeled and diced
4	tablespoons olive oil
1	tablespoon vinegar
¼-½	cup green chiles, diced (use canned or fresh, depending upon how hot you like it)
	dash of white wine
	tortillas or crackers

✳ Combine the trout and lemon juice in a non-reactive bowl, and marinate overnight in the refrigerator.

✳ Two hours before serving, combine the minced onion, tomato, olive oil, vinegar, green chiles, and white wine in a serving bowl. Drain the lemon juice from the trout, and add the trout to the serving bowl. Discard the lemon juice. Chill.

✳ Serve as a dip with tortillas or crackers. Serves 6.

r. scott phillips

As managing director of the Utah Shakespearean Festival, R. Scott Phillips shares responsibility for budgeting and personnel, and for developing the Festival into a highly successful endeavor. During his sixteen years at the Festival, the annual operating budget has grown from $329,000 to over $3 million. Each summer, thousands of people converge on Cedar City to participate in the many renaissance festivities and to see three Shakespearean productions, rotating nightly. A bachelor, Scott says he is "married" to his job, but has a large theater family and many godchildren.

Her Majesty's Pasta

After a long day of juggling my duties at my gift boutique, Her Majesty Shoppe, and the Shakespearean Festival, this dish is a quick and healthy meal. Best of all, the clean up is minimal.

1	pound angel hair pasta
¼	cup olive oil
4-6	garlic cloves, minced
1	cup sun-dried tomatoes soaked in oil, drained, and chopped
4	ounces Proscuitto ham (optional), sliced thin
1	cup fresh basil, slivered
¼	cup pine nuts
	freshly ground black pepper, to taste
	freshly grated Parmesan cheese

☀ Bring a large pot of water to a boil for the pasta.

☀ Place the garlic and olive oil in a glass bowl. Microwave on medium-high for 3-4 minutes, or until the garlic begins to brown.

☀ Meanwhile, add the pasta to the water. Cook at a rolling boil until the pasta is al dente, about 2 minutes. Drain. Transfer the pasta to a warmed pasta bowl.

☀ Add the sun-dried tomatoes, proscuitto ham, and fresh basil to the olive oil-garlic mixture. Pour over the pasta. Top with pine nuts, black pepper and Parmesan cheese. Serves 4.

pete plastow

Pete Plastow's life has been a collage of places and careers. Born in Florida into an Army family, Pete was raised all over the country. He joined the Marines after high school, then worked as a cowboy before going on to college. He graduated with a degree in animal husbandry. That led him to a string of jobs as a herdsman and foreman. He decided to take a steady job with the New York State Museum in Albany. Eleven years later, Pete decided he'd had enough of the East and wanted to turn his favorite pursuit, painting, into a vocation. He, his wife, Patt, and their six children moved back to his heartland, Moab. The first few years weren't easy but with much dedication Pete's art gained popularity. He is now shown in galleries across the country and placed in private art collections around the world. The rich fabric of Pete's diverse life gives the artist tremendous depth.

Chocolate Peppermint Pie

Here is a quick recipe for an old-time favorite.

1	8-inch pie crust, baked
1	11.5-ounce package semi-sweet chocolate chips
2	tablespoons granulated sugar
3	tablespoons milk
4	eggs, separated
1	teaspoon vanilla extract
1	pint heavy or whipping cream, whipped
2-3	peppermint sticks

 In a double boiler, combine the chocolate chips, sugar, and milk, and cook over medium-low heat until the chips have melted. Cool.

☀ Add the egg yolks, one at a time, to the chocolate mixture, and beat well. Add the vanilla, and stir in. Beat the egg whites until stiff, and fold into the chocolate mixture.

☀ Fill the pie crust with the chocolate mixture, and chill for 2 hours.

☀ Before serving, top the pie with fresh whipped cream. In a plastic bag, crush the peppermint sticks, and sprinkle over whipped cream. Serve and stand back. Serves 8.

dave
porter

For many years, Dave Porter provided a vital link between Utahns and what happened on Utah's highways, in its governmental chambers and anywhere else news occurred. As a radio news anchor, news director, writer, reporter, and press secretary for Senator Orrin Hatch, he was on the front lines of breaking news. Today, Dave is the director of publicity for the Utah Travel Council and is still seen on television and heard on the radio promoting tourism in the state. He is a native of Utah and, says he has stayed, because of the state's "changing seasons, diversity, and, golf courses." Dave resides in Kaysville with his wife and five children.

Greatest Lasagna in Utah

"My lasagna recipe was influenced by a friend of mine from Naples, Italy. The recipe has evolved over the past 22 years while making it for hundreds of friends. I like it spicy; you may not. You can experiment. My lasagna was really put to the test at the Governor's Mansion a few years ago. I prepared it for the Governor's staff Christmas party. The First Lady, Norma Matheson, said it was the best she had ever eaten."

6	16-ounce cans tomato sauce
1	tablespoon dried oregano
1	tablespoon dried sweet basil
1	tablespoon dried rosemary
2	teaspoons salt
2	teaspoons pepper
10	hot or mild sausages, diced
1	garlic clove, sliced thin
1	pound lasagna noodles
2	15-ounce containers ricotta cheese (don't use cottage cheese)
1	pound Mozzarella cheese, grated

☀ In a large pot, combine the tomato sauce with the oregano, sweet basil, rosemary, salt and pepper and bring to a boil. Lower the heat and simmer for at least 5 hours. The longer the sauce cooks, the better the flavor. Meanwhile, sauté the sausage in its own fat until browned. Drain, and add the sausage to the sauce during the first hour of simmering. It is very important to stir the sauce often to avoid burning the bottom of the pot.

☀ Preheat oven to 350°.

☀ Bring a large pot of water to a boil. Add the lasagna noodles, and a little oil, and cook until al dente, about 10 minutes. Drain, rinse noodles under cold water, drain again, and separate the noodles to keep them from sticking.

☀ Now you are ready to build your lasagna in a 9x13-inch pan. First, drizzle some of the sauce in the bottom of the pan. Add a layer of noodles, more sauce, and a layer of the cheeses. Repeat for 3-4 layers, depending upon the depth of your pan. The top layer should be sauce and cheese.

☀ Bake for 30 minutes and let it sit for 10 minutes before serving. Serves 8.

heidi preuss

The little girl in the photo with the taller-than-her ski poles was destined for greatness. At fifteen years old, Heidi Preuss was ranked seventeenth in the world in the alpine slalom event. She remained ranked in the top thirty in one of several alpine events for over ten years. The highlight of Heidi's career was a fourth-place finish in the downhill event in the 1980 Winter Olympics in Lake Placid, N.Y. While numerous injuries (not all related to skiing) interrupted her career, Heidi says emphatically that she would do it all over again.

"The drive and the challenge of working to be the best in the world taught me more in the way of values and inner balance than anything else I could have done. Skiing is a joy and at that level of ability, the world feels like yours. It is not just a sport but a quest to become greater than oneself, to learn and push the limits of your ability."

Heidi lives with her husband, Terry, in Salt Lake City.

Olive Stuffed Leg of Lamb

"Roast leg of lamb with mint sauce is about as boring as meat can be. This recipe from my mom has lots of scrumptious taste. Enjoy the mix of flavors, the strength of which is dictated by the amount of olives and garlic you choose to use."

1	7-pound leg of lamb
2	tablespoons dry ginger
1	tablespoon dry mustard
1	teaspoon salt
1	teaspoon freshly ground pepper
3	slices bacon, chopped into ½-inch pieces
8	ounces stuffed green olives, or more to taste
3	cloves garlic, or more to taste
1	cup butter (1 stick)
1	cup Burgundy wine
1	cup water

☀ Preheat oven to 450°.

☀ Cut excess fat from the leg of lamb. Cut several 2-inch deep slits into the lamb.

☀ In a small bowl, combine the ginger, mustard, salt, and pepper. Add the bacon to the spice mixture, and coat thoroughly.

☀ Slice each garlic clove into 8 pieces. Do not mince.

☀ Into the slits of the lamb, stuff a piece of bacon, a piece of garlic, and an olive, followed again by garlic and bacon. The number of stuffed slits will determine the intensity of the flavor.

☀ After stuffing all the olives, bacon, and garlic into the lamb, rub the leg with the butter.

☀ Place the meat on a roasting pan and roast for 20 minutes.

☀ Remove the meat from the oven, and pour the Burgundy wine and water over the leg. Reduce the heat to 350° and roast for 1 hour more for medium-rare. Let sit for 15 minutes before slicing. Serves 8.

john price

Developer John Price's entrepreneurial nature surfaced at an early age. When he was eight years old, he used a converted wagon to deliver groceries from local grocery stores to neighborhood apartment houses. Today, the Salt Lake City businessman is the nation's thirty-fifth largest lessor of shopping center space, has built fourteen malls, and owns two local radio stations. John, whose Jewish family fled Nazi Germany before World War II, says he wants to give something back to the country that has been so good to him. He is a generous contributor to political campaigns and volunteers on many community boards.

John's Pasta Delight!

1	cup shell pasta
1	pound ground beef
1	medium onion, chopped
½	green bell pepper, chopped
1	stalk celery, chopped on the diagonal
1	teaspoon turmeric
1	teaspoon thyme
1	10¾-ounce can tomato soup
2	8-ounce cans tomato sauce
1	8-ounce can corn
	salt and pepper, to taste
½	cup Cheddar cheese, grated

☀ Preheat oven to 350°.

☀ Bring a pot of water to a boil. Add the pasta shells, and cook at a rolling boil until al dente, about 8-10 minutes. Drain.

☀ In a skillet, combine the ground beef, onion, bell pepper, and celery. Cook over medium heat until the beef is browned, about 8 minutes. Drain liquid. Stir in turmeric, and thyme.

☀ In a large casserole, combine the pasta shells, ground beef mixture, tomato soup, tomato sauce, corn, and salt and pepper. Top with the Cheddar cheese.

☀ Bake the casserole for 30 minutes.

☀ Serve with tossed green salad, fresh green beans, crusty French bread, and a glass of Chenin Blanc. Serves 8-10.

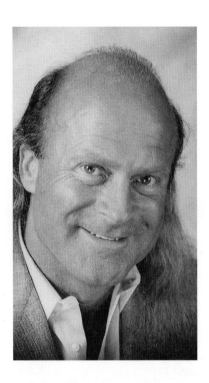

Summmum Bonum Amon Ra, "Corky" to his friends, may be Utah's most unusual entrepreneur. Born in Salt Lake City and educated at the University of Utah, Corky is the founder of the first licensed winery in the state. In a forty-foot-high pyramid in Salt Lake City, Corky makes sacramental wine for sale to religious groups. And Corky offers clients the opportunity to be preserved for eternity with his modern day "Mummification" technique. He has patented the process and registered the word as a trademark. Corky is also the founder of the Summum, a philosophical organization, and has authored two books. Corky lives with his wife, Gracey, four cats, and two Doberman pinschers, (one cat and one dog are mummies) in the shadow of their pyramid winery.

Corky's Cajun Salmon

"This salmon is not only tasty, it's ready in less than 15 minutes. You can use any Cajun blackening spice, but I prefer Authentic Cajun Dust."

1	2-pound salmon fillet, cut in half
2-4	tablespoons of your favorite Cajun blackening spice
⅓	cup olive oil

☀ Place the salmon on waxed paper, and sprinkle the blackening spice on the flesh side of each salmon fillet. Coat the salmon according to how spicy you like your food.

☀ Heat the olive oil in an electric skillet or heavy fry pan until the temperature reaches 420°, or until the oil just begins to smoke. Place the salmon fillet in the hot oil, skin-side down. Cover and sear the skin-side of the salmon for 1½-2 minutes. Turn off the heat and carefully flip the fillets. With a fork, remove the skin and season this side of the fillet according to taste. Turn the heat back to 420°, cover, and sear this side for another 1½-2 minutes. The Cajun blackening spice should be brown on both sides when finished, but **not** black. Serve with your favorite sourdough bread and green salad. Serves 2.

greg ragland

Greg Ragland didn't fit in at Arizona State University's architecture department. His professors deemed his ideas and drawings too wild. Greg found his niche quite by accident when they sent him to the art department. Greg went on to graduate number one in his class. From college, Greg and his wife, Hollie, moved to New York City where he quickly proved his conceptual ability. He has illustrated for **Money, Sports Illustrated, Time, Newsweek, GQ,** *and* **Fortune** *magazines and done many book covers. Today, he is recognized as one of the best editorial illustrators in the country. The Raglands moved from New York to Park City, as Greg says, "to get our kids a yard and some open space."*

Mema's Hot Rolls

"My grandmother, Mema, cooked this longtime family recipe for gatherings at Christmas, Thanksgiving and reunions."

1	tablespoon (1 package) active dry yeast
1	cup warm water
¼	cup Crisco
¼	cup granulated sugar
1	teaspoon salt
1	egg
3½	cups all-purpose flour, or more, if needed
	butter or margarine for dipping

☼ Stir yeast into warm water and let stand 5 minutes.

☼ Blend together Crisco, sugar, salt and the egg in a small bowl. In a large bowl, combine yeast and water, egg mixture, and flour, and mix thoroughly for 2 minutes with a wooden spoon.

☼ Turn the dough onto a lightly floured surface and knead the dough for about 6 minutes. Add more flour, if needed, to make the dough smooth and elastic.

☼ Shape the dough into a ball and turn it into a greased bowl. Cover the bowl and let the dough rise in a warm place until it has doubled in size.

☼ Preheat oven to 400° and butter 2 twelve-cup muffin tins.

☼ Punch the dough down, and divide into 48 small balls. Roll each ball in butter or margarine. Place 2 balls, side by side, in each cup of a buttered muffin tin. Cover loosely and let the dough rise, and double in size again.

☼ Bake 12 minutes until tops are golden brown. Makes 2 dozen rolls.

tony rasmussen

Anton "Tony" Rasmussen's studies in biology and chemistry, and his familiarity with the microscopic world of cells, sensitized him to the abstract patterns inherent in the visible world. That sensitivity is reflected in his painting, which balance both his interests in traditional and nontraditional ways of interpreting the world. His depiction of Utah's landmarks—Delicate Arch, Lake Powell, Dead Horse Point, the Great White Throne and others— were Salt Lake International Airport's first art acquisitions. Seven enormous murals hang in the airport. His paintings of Utah scenes also grace the cover and interior of this cookbook. Tony and his wife, Pamela, live in Salt Lake City with their daughter, Ariel, who, Tony says, is the apple of her father's eye and the undisputed boss of the Rasmussen family.

Broccoli Ham Quiche

A splash of balsamic vinegar and a bit of Parmesan cheese lends a uniquely sweet yet tangy taste to this classic quiche.

1	package pie crust pastry
1	bunch broccoli
1	cup heavy cream
1	cup milk
4	eggs
½	cup chopped ham
¾	cup Swiss cheese, grated
1	tablespoon balsamic vinegar
	salt and freshly ground pepper, to taste
¼	cup grated Parmesan cheese

☀ Preheat oven to 375°. Line a 9-inch quiche dish with pie crust pastry.

☀ Remove the stems from the broccoli, and cut the tops into small pieces. Bring a pot of salted water to a boil, and blanch the broccoli for 5 minutes. Drain, cool and chop coarsely. You should have approximately 2 cups.

☀ In a mixing bowl, whisk together the cream, milk, and eggs. Stir in the broccoli, ham, Swiss cheese, and balsamic vinegar. Season with salt and pepper, to taste.

☀ Pour the egg and cheese mixture into the pastry-lined quiche dish. Sprinkle the Parmesan cheese over the quiche.

☀ Bake for 30 minutes, or until puffed and golden. Serves 6.

helen reddy

Of the many honors Helen Reddy has received, she is most proud of a reddish-violet tulip the Dutch named for her. Helen is indeed a wonder of nature. Born into a well-known Australian show business family, Helen has been performing professionally since she was a child. Her remarkably clear, precise voice and her genius for songwriting have generated many gold- and platinum-selling albums and top ten singles, including **I Am Woman, Leave Me Alone,** *and* **You and Me Against the World.** *Helen is active in community affairs. Her fans in Utah are devoted and when she sang for Salt Lake City's YWCA fundraising concert, Abravanel Hall was sold out.*

Three Chocolate Scones

2	cups all-purpose flour
1/4	cup packed brown sugar
1/4	teaspoon baking soda
1 1/2	teaspoons baking powder
1/4	cup unsalted butter, cut into 1/2-inch cubes
1/2	cup buttermilk
2	egg whites
1 1/2	teaspoons vanilla extract
2	ounces bittersweet chocolate, cut into 1/2-inch pieces
2	ounces milk chocolate, cut into 1/2-inch pieces
2	ounces white chocolate, cut into 1/2-inch pieces

☀ Preheat oven to 375°.

☀ In a large mixing bowl, stir together the flour, brown sugar, baking soda, and baking powder. Add the butter pieces. Cut in the butter using two knives until the mixture resembles large bread crumbs.

☀ In a small mixing bowl, stir together the buttermilk, egg whites, and vanilla extract.

☀ Add the buttermilk mixture to the flour mixture. Stir to combine. Stir in the chocolate pieces until they are evenly distributed.

☀ Drop the dough onto an ungreased baking sheet, using a 1/4 cup measuring cup. Leave two inches between each scone.

☀ Bake until the tops are lightly browned, and a toothpick inserted in the middle comes out clean, about 25 minutes.

☀ Remove the baking sheet from the oven, and place on a wire rack to cool for 5 minutes. Then, using a spatula, remove the scones from the baking sheet, and place directly on the wire rack until ready to serve.

☀ Serve the warm scones with butter. Makes 10-12 scones.

robert redford

*It took Robert Redford four years to set up the Sundance Film Institute. During those intense years in the early 1980s, Bob went without acting or directing, choosing to devote his time to an ideal. The Institute's Sundance Film Festival, held each January in Park City, is the biggest market for independent film in the world. Bob conceived the Festival to be an alternative to Hollywood, a creative lab for filmmaking not driven by a bottom line. He has embraced the same uncompromising position in his choice of projects. While **A River Runs Through It** and **Quiz Show**, movies Bob developed and directed, were both commercial successes, they surpassed Hollywood films in subject and depth. The Sundance Film Institute is headquartered at another Redford creation, Sundance, a year-round community committed to the harmonious alliance of recreation and arts.*

Foil Baked Utah Trout

Sundance chef Don Heidel contributes this recipe from the Tree Room for Robert Redford. The Tree Room is an elegantly rustic restaurant serving fresh, unique entrées. Often, the food is locally produced or grown at the resort.

5	Utah trout, whole and deboned
10	cherry tomatoes, halved
1	potato, sliced very thin
1	carrot, peeled, and cut into julienne
1	portabello mushroom, thinly sliced
3	asparagus stalks, cut on the diagonal into 1-inch pieces
½	zucchini, thinly sliced
½	yellow squash, thinly sliced
	salt and pepper, to taste

Pear Butter:

½	cup butter
½	ripe pear
	salt and pepper, to taste

☀ To prepare the Pear Butter: Blend the butter, pear, and salt and pepper together in a food processor until smooth.

☀ Preheat oven to 350°.

☀ To prepare the trout: Butterfly or open the trout so it lays flat. Spread the pear butter over the trout meat. Season with salt and pepper. Layer a fifth of the vegetables over the pear butter. Repeat with remaining trout. Close up each trout and wrap in foil, taking care not to punch holes in the tin foil.

☀ Bake fish for approximately 15 minutes. Alternatively, the trout may be cooked over an open fire for 15 minutes. Serves 5.

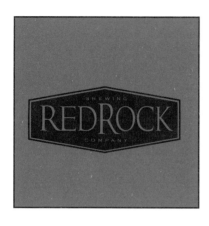

redrock
brewing
company

93

Located in downtown Salt Lake City, the RedRock Brewing Company has not been able to sate the local thirst. But that is only because there is an unremitting demand for the ten beers RedRock brews. Once an empty warehouse, the 250-seat brew pub is almost always packed and its stainless steel vats, which are capable of brewing 310 gallons at a time, are always producing. From German wheat beers, to Scottish ales, to oatmeal stouts, the 10-barrel brewery is quickly gaining a reputation for producing some of the best quaffs in Utah. With its exposed ceilings, open windows, mellow woods, and brick interior, RedRock is also becoming known as the place to be seen in Salt Lake City.

RedRock Wheat Pancakes

Head brewer Eric Dunlap sends this recipe from the RedRock kitchen, where contemporary American fare is created.

1 ¼	cups whole wheat flour
¾	cup white flour
1	teaspoon salt
3	tablespoons granulated sugar
1	teaspoon baking powder
3	eggs
1	cup milk
3	cups RedRock Hefe-Weizen
	butter or margarine for cooking the pancakes

☀ In a large mixing bowl, stir together the dry ingredients. Separate the eggs, and set the whites aside. Add the egg yolks, milk, and beer to the flour mixture. Stir until free of lumps. In a medium bowl, whip the egg whites until stiff. Fold the egg whites into the batter.

☀ Heat the griddle over medium-high heat, and then coat the griddle with butter or margarine. Spoon 2-3 table-spoons of batter onto the griddle, and cook until the bottom of the pancake is golden, and bubbles are breaking on the top. Turn the pancakes, and cook for another few minutes. Repeat, using all of the batter. Makes 1 dozen 3- to 4-inch pancakes.

rim tours

After pedaling through the Utah backcountry along canyon rims, through streams and over hills, the deluxe camp that Rim Tours has set up ahead looks awfully inviting. Started in 1985 and based in Moab, Rim Tours offers mountain bike enthusiasts the trip of their lifetime through some of the most awe-inspiring scenery available on two wheels, or on foot for that matter. Mountain bike riders from all over the world come to the famous slickrock trails around Moab. Owners Kirstin Peterson and Matt Hebberd have extensive cycling backgrounds and offer bike adventures at Moab, Canyonlands National Park, the Colorado Rockies, and Arizona.

Dutch Oven Salmon

After years of guiding bicycle tours, Rim Tours has learned that good healthy food doesn't have to be bland. This hearty recipe, developed by guide Scott Escott, is often served with Dutch oven roasted red and sweet potatoes and a green salad.

4	salmon fillets, about 6 ounces each
1	medium yellow onion
½	cup Dijon mustard
½	cup mayonnaise (you may use low-fat)
½	cup fresh Parmesan cheese, grated
	fresh ground pepper

☀ Wash the salmon fillets and pat dry. Oil the bottom of a 12-inch Dutch oven. Ignite about 25 charcoal briquettes.

☀ Dice the onions and mix with Dijon mustard, mayonnaise, and Parmesan cheese.

☀ Place the fish skin-side down in the oiled Dutch oven, taking care not to overlap the fish. Spread the sauce over the fish and grind the pepper over the top of the sauce. Cover.

☀ When the charcoal is gray, arrange a piece of aluminum foil on the ground or in the fire pan. Place 4-5 briquettes in a small circle on the foil. Place the Dutch oven on the charcoal circle. Put the remaining coals around the edge of the lid of the Dutch oven, placing 3-4 in the middle of the lid. It's that easy. But, keep out of the wind.

☀ Bake for 45-60 minutes, or until fish is barely opaque. Do not overcook. Use channel locks to lift the hot lid to test doneness.

☀ Alternatively, you can bake the fish in the oven at 375° for 20 minutes. Serves 4.

carmen rogers

Carmen Rogers is the Martha Stewart (minus the hype) of Utah. She is a tastemaster, who is sought out to design and furnish the most elegant Utah interiors. Unlike Martha, she doesn't own chickens. But the Canadian native and Park City resident's culinary skills are so acclaimed that a dinner she once created to auction at a KPCW fundraiser earned $1,800 for the local public radio station. Carmen's husband, Rick, is a former actor, who played a medic on the television series **Combat,** *and, during the 1960s, acted in many other television series. He is active in Save Our Stage, a grassroots group committed to restoring Park City's Egyptian Theater, an art deco structure built in the 1920s.*

Autumn Vegetable Medley

"When I moved to Los Angeles from Montreal twenty-five years ago, I befriended a lady who had also just moved to LA and whose background was Mormon. She gave me this vegetable recipe which has become a favorite. I think it's fitting that it should return to Utah. It's delicious with pork, chicken, or turkey. Best of all, it can be made ahead of time."

¾	pound rutabagas
3	large carrots
¾	pound yams
¾	cup unsalted butter
⅛	teaspoon ground nutmeg
	salt and pepper to taste

☀ Preheat oven to 375°.

☀ Peel the rutabagas, carrots, and yams, and cut into 1-inch chunks.

☀ Place the vegetables in a pan, and cover with water. Bring to a boil, and cook over high heat until tender when pierced, about 25 minutes. Drain.

☀ Put the vegetables back on the burner briefly and let the moisture evaporate.

☀ In a food processor or food mill, mix together the vegetables, butter, nutmeg, and salt and pepper until smooth.

☀ Spoon into a 1- to 1½-quart shallow casserole dish. Bake uncovered until hot, about 30 minutes. Serves 6.

kenny rogers

*Kenny Rogers epitomizes the
American rags-to-riches story. Born
in a housing project in Houston,
Kenny says he grew up poor but
happy. When he was thirteen and
sick in bed with the measles, he
taught himself to play the guitar. An
"A" student in high school, he sang
in the glee club and church choir.
After graduating (he was the first
member of his family to complete
high school), he joined the New
Christy Minstrels, and left that
group to form the First Edition. The
rest is history. His album, **The
Gambler**, went triple platinum.
Kenny continues to set attendance
records at concerts across the country. When **People** magazine polled
a group of women recently, they
listed Kenny as one of their top ten
favorite celebrities. Getting away
from it for Kenny is a sunset cruise
on Lake Powell on his boat, appro-
priately named, The Gambler.*

Chicken Salad à la Rogers

"I am pleased to share one of my very favorite recipes with
you. This is a delicious chicken salad for luncheons and light
suppers. Guests love it as well."

2	cups cooked chicken (white meat)
3	dill pickles (non-kosher)
½	cup chopped walnuts
¼	cup slivered or chopped almonds
	salt and pepper, to taste
	chopped scallions, optional
	lettuce

 Pull the chicken from the bone, rather than cutting it.
Tear into bite-size pieces. Peel the pickles with a potato
peeler, and chop. Mix all of the above ingredients lightly
with a salad dressing of your choice. You may also want
to add chopped scallions. Season to taste and serve on
a bed of fresh, crisp lettuce.

We suggest a Mustard-Dill-Chive Vinaigrette for this salad.

Vinaigrette:

1	tablespoon Dijon mustard
1	tablespoon minced shallots
1	tablespoon minced fresh chives
1	tablespoon chopped fresh dill, or ½ tablespoon dried
¼	cup vinegar (tarragon, red wine or homemade flavored vinegar)
½	cup olive oil
	salt and fresh ground pepper, to taste

 Place the mustard in a small bowl. Add the shallots,
chives, dill, and vinegar and blend lightly. Drizzle in the
olive oil, whisking constantly until the dressing has
thickened. Fold in the salt and fresh ground pepper. Let
the dressing sit, covered, for about 20 minutes before
serving. Serves 4.

dick roth

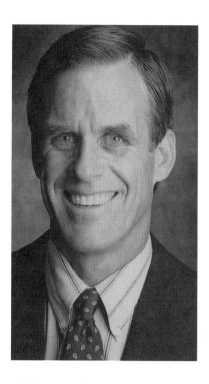

Chocolate Lover's Hot Fudge Sauce

"This is my mom's famous recipe, and my favorite. Extra sauce can be refrigerated. If it crystallizes, simply microwave until soft and the crystals disappear."

2	cups granulated sugar
¾	cup milk
2-4	squares unsweetened chocolate, depending upon your level of chocoholism
¾	cube (6 tablespoons) butter
1	tablespoon corn syrup
	a pinch of salt
1	teaspoon vanilla extract

 In a double boiler, dissolve the sugar in the milk over medium heat. Add the chocolate squares and cook until melted. Add the butter and melt, and mix well. Stir in the corn syrup and a pinch of salt. Stir a little as the sauce thickens, but don't disturb it too much. You want to cook the chocolate until it is at the soft ball stage. In other words, cook until a drop of hot chocolate in cool water makes a soft ball. If you cook it longer, the sauce will harden on the ice cream, which can be fun. When cooked to desired stage, add the vanilla and heat through. Cool for a minute before serving on your favorite ice cream. Makes 3½ cups.

Either stupid or courageous. That's how Dick Roth describes his decision to swim in the 1964 Olympics. The day before the trials, Dick was struck with acute appendicitis. He refused emergency surgery. "The doctors filled me full of antibiotics, packed my stomach in ice, put me on a liquid diet, kept me in isolation, and watched my white blood count." Sick and in pain, Dick barely qualified, but two days later, he won the gold and set a world record in the individual medley, swimming's decathlon. Both he and his appendix are enshrined in the International Swimming Hall of Fame. A successful entrepreneur, Dick currently lives in Park City and is a consultant and presenter at the Covey Leadership Center.

stefene russell

Stefene Russell is a native of Salt Lake City, where she grew up in a house built by polygamists and haunted by ghosts of the same. The house can be seen in the film **Plan 10 From Outer Space,** *a Trent Harris sci-fi comedy, in which she plays the lead. She also acted in* **The Backward Swing,** *where she swung on a trapeze over a plaster volcano, and David Brother's* **Space Boss,** *where she recited T. Rex's lyrics in a field of wheat. Currently, Stefene is writing for* **Twitch, The Event, Catalyst,** *and* **Salt Lake City** *magazines, as well as national magazines.* **Mademoiselle** *recently featured her article on Mormon feminists. She also reads her poetry in local venues such as Sam Weller's Zion Bookstore and the CityArt Reading Series.*

William Blake Cake or "The Marriage of Heaven and Hell" Manifested in Dessert Form

Angel Food Cake:

1	cup cake flour, sifted
1½	cups superfine granulated sugar, divided in half
¼	teaspoon salt
12	large egg whites, at room temperature
1	teaspoon cream of tartar
2	teaspoons vanilla extract
½	teaspoon almond extract
1	teaspoon freshly-squeezed lemon juice

Devil's Food Cake:

4	ounces (8 tablespoons) bittersweet chocolate squares
6	tablespoons butter, at room temperature
6	tablespoons unsweetened cocoa powder
1	cup unsalted butter
½	cup dark brown sugar, packed
¼	cup sour cream
2	teaspoons baking soda
2	teaspoons boiling water
1½	cups all-purpose flour, sifted
3	tablespoons granulated sugar
6	egg whites
	cherry compote

To prepare the Angel Food Cake:

☀ Preheat oven to 350°.

☀ In a small mixing bowl, combine the cake flour, ¾ cup sugar, and salt.

☀ In a separate mixing bowl, whip the egg whites on low speed until slightly frothy. Add cream of tartar, and continue whipping until egg whites mound. Increase the speed to medium, and slowly add the remaining ¾ cup sugar, 2 tablespoons at a time. Continue whipping until egg whites are stiff but not dry. Beat in vanilla extract, almond extract, and fresh lemon juice.

☀ Gently fold the dry ingredients into the egg whites, 3 tablespoons at a time.

Pour the batter into an ungreased ring-shaped pan, and tap to remove bubbles. Bake until the cake is golden brown and springs back when lightly touched, about 40 minutes. Remove the cake from the pan by running a thin-bladed knife around the inside of the pan. Let cool and invert the cake onto a plate.

To prepare the Devil's Food Cake:

Preheat oven to 350°. Butter a ring-shaped pan and lightly dust with cocoa.

Break the chocolate squares apart, and melt in a double boiler. Set aside.

In a small saucepan, melt the 6 tablespoons butter, and whisk in the cocoa powder. Bring to a simmer over medium heat, whisking constantly until smooth and thickened. Stir in the melted chocolate squares, and set aside.

In large a mixing bowl, beat 1 cup unsalted butter until it peaks and whitens. Beat in the brown sugar and sour cream.

Dissolve the baking soda in the boiling water and set aside to fizz.

To the butter-sour cream mixture, beat in half of the flour. Add the baking soda mixture, and beat in the remaining flour. Set aside.

Beat the egg whites on low-speed until frothy, then on medium until peaks form. Increase the speed to high, and beat in the granulated sugar until stiff glossy peaks form. Whisk half of the egg whites into the chocolate mixture, and fold in the rest. Fold in the sour cream mixture.

Pour the batter into the prepared ring-shaped pan and bake until the cake shrinks slightly from sides and springs back when touched, about 25 minutes. Turn upside down on a plate and cool.

To Prepare the William Blake Cake:

Cut both cakes in half on the horizontal. On a long platter, recombine each half so that you have two new cakes, each one-half angel and one-half devil's. Place the cakes side-by-side so they form an infinity symbol.

Cover the cake with cherry compote, which will not clash with either cake. This is a good birthday cake for Geminis, or those on restricted diets for the sake of their hearts or waistlines.

Temples and Towers of the Virgin, Panel 3

100

The "buzz" in Utah is all about the Salt Lake Buzz. More than 1.5 million people have watched the dynamic baseball team play at Salt Lake City's Franklin Quest Field since it was built in 1994. Veteran Manager Phil Roof directed the Triple-A affiliate of the Minnesota Twins to the championship series in 1995. Phil has been in baseball for thirty years, both as a player and manager in the major and minor leagues, and has worked in cities from the East Coast to the West Coast and from the Gulf of Mexico to Toronto. Phil says that in all his travels, he has never played nor managed in a town quite as nice, clean, and pretty as Salt Lake City.

Vegetable Seafood Medley

General Manager Phil Roof contributes this recipe on behalf of the team. He says, "This is a versatile recipe because you can add or subtract ingredients according to the availability of fresh vegetables."

1	pound linguine
½	cup clam juice, divided
4	tablespoons olive oil, divided
1	carrot, peeled and cut into julienne
1	small yellow squash, seeded and cut into julienne
1	small zucchini, cut on the diagonal into ¼-inch thick pieces
1	medium onion, slivered
1	small head cauliflower, trimmed and cut into florets
1	small head broccoli, trimmed and cut into florets
½	pound fresh mushrooms, thinly sliced
1	teaspoon garlic salt
1	teaspoon Dash seasoning
2	pounds shrimp, peeled, and deveined; or 2 pounds scallops; or 2 dozen clams, shucked; or a combination
3	tomatoes, diced

❀ For the pasta, bring a large pot of water to a boil.

❀ Combine ¼ cup clam juice and 2 tablespoons olive oil in a skillet. Add the carrot, squash, zucchini, onion, cauliflower, broccoli, and mushrooms over medium heat and sauté until cooked through but not browned, about 8 minutes. Season with garlic salt and Dash seasoning.

❀ In a separate skillet, combine the remaining ¼ cup clam juice and 2 tablespoons olive oil and heat over medium. Sauté the shrimp, scallops, or clams (or a combination) until cooked through, about 2-3 minutes.

❀ Meanwhile, add the linguine to the boiling water, and cook at a rolling boil until pasta is al dente, about 6-8 minutes. Drain.

❀ Combine the seafood with the vegetables, stir, and heat through. Pour the linguine into a warm serving bowl, and top with the vegetable-seafood medley. Garnish with tomatoes and serve immediately. Serves 8.

todd schlopy

Ten years ago a handsome football player followed a beautiful skier to Utah. They landed in Park City and the rest is the stuff of fairy tales. Todd Schlopy became a first assistant cameraman for such films as **The Stand** *and* **Homeward Bound-The Incredible Journey.** *The former Seattle Seahawks' place kicker also founded Action Sports Management, an agency representing winter sport athletes. The beautiful woman, who was a two-time Olympian, consented to be his wife (see Holly Flanders). Together, they have two sweet, smart children, and will live happily ever after among the aspen and snow flakes of Utah.*
The End.

Fifty-Five Yard French Toast

"This is a French toast recipe with a kick. Maple syrup and vanilla in the batter, and ground cinnamon as a final touch are guaranteed to produce fifty- to sixty-yard field goals. I got through five years at the University of Michigan, two Rose Bowls, a Sugar Bowl, and a Bluebonnet Bowl on a stack of this stuff almost every morning. Enjoy."

2	large or extra-large eggs
2-3	tablespoons milk
3	tablespoons maple syrup
½	teaspoon pure vanilla extract
4	slices bread (stale French bread, sourdough, white, whole wheat, etc.)
	oil or butter for cooking French toast

✺ Set the griddle or fry pan to medium-high heat. Beat eggs, milk, maple syrup, and vanilla together in a mixing bowl until maple syrup is thoroughly dissolved into the batter. Soak bread on both sides—the longer the soak, the creamier the center.

✺ Heat oil or butter in the griddle. Place bread directly onto hot griddle, turning once to brown each side. Sprinkle finished stack with ground cinnamon. Serve hot with butter or margarine, and warm New England maple syrup.

✺ Low-Fat Option: Substitute 3 eggs whites and one yolk. Use Skim milk. Use low-cal syrup (in the batter only). Serves 1-2.

102

Seven Wives Inn holds some secrets worth investigating. Located in St. George's historical district, the bed and breakfast consists of two neighboring pioneer homes. Edwin G. Woolley built the larger house in 1873. He constructed a secret door that led to the attic, where he hid polygamists from federal marshals. One of those polygamists, Benjamin F. Johnson, a relative of the innkeeper, had seven wives, hence the name. The inn is decorated with period furnishings and the full breakfast served each morning is definitely worth an extra day stayover. Killer waffles, apple-pecan pancakes, and eggs Mornay, or some tantalizing dishes that guests can't keep secret.

The Fifth Wife's Sausage En Croute

This dish can be partially prepared the night before, so there's very little left to do in the morning.

Filling:

1	pound bulk sausage
1	tablespoon butter
4	green onions, chopped, including some green tops
6	mushrooms, cleaned and sliced thin
½	cup Monterey Jack cheese, grated

Crust:

½	cup butter
¾	cup cottage cheese
1	cup all-purpose flour

☀ To prepare the filling: Heat the butter in a large sauté pan, and add the onions and mushrooms. Sauté until limp and set aside. To the same pan, add the sausage and cook until no longer pink. Refrigerate each in separate containers until morning.

☀ To prepare the crust: In a food processor, blend the butter and cottage cheese leaving some pea-size butter pieces. Add the flour and pulse the machine until just blended. Form the dough into a ball, wrap in plastic wrap, and refrigerate overnight or for at least two hours.

☀ In the morning, preheat oven to 350°. Roll out the dough into a long oval. Spoon the sausage down the center length of the dough and top with the mushroom and onion mixture. Sprinkle cheese on top. Make about six slashes in the crust from the edge towards the center, and then lap the crust, weaving and overlapping the strands over the filling. Pinch the dough closed, and gently place on a cookie sheet. Bake for 30 minutes or until golden brown. Serves 6-8.

margaret mary shuff

When Margaret Mary Shuff and husband John started **Salt Lake City** *magazine in 1989, they thought that Utah would be their secondary residence. The couple lived in Boca Raton, Florida, where they had created* **Boca Raton** *magazine. They continue to publish the award-winning Florida magazine, but they've become westerners, moving their primary residence to Park City.* **Salt Lake City** *magazine has thrived as well. The sophisticated, four-color magazine has received many industry awards and subscriptions have steadily grown, making it the magazine of the Mountain West. Margaret Mary praises Utah, calling it "the best kept secret in the country."*

Blinis with Caviar

A woman able to improvise and adapt, Margaret Mary tells us, "I once had some great smoked salmon and nothing to serve it with. So, I thought fresh dill and corn pancake mix would make a wonderful blini to accompany the salmon. Here's my creation."

1	package corn pancake mix
2-3	tablespoons chopped fresh dill weed
	oil for cooking blinis
	sour cream and caviar, for garnish
	or
	plain yogurt and mustard, for garnish
	smoked salmon

☀ To the package of corn pancake mix, add the dill weed and prepare according to the instructions.

☀ Lightly grease a griddle with oil, and place it over medium heat. Drop the batter by tablespoons onto the hot griddle, and cook until bubbles form on top and the undersides are golden, about 1 minute. Flip, and cook for 1 more minute.

☀ Serve immediately with a dollop of sour cream and caviar or a dollop of yogurt and mustard. Top with smoked salmon.

THE GREATEST SNOW
ON EARTH

104

*Ski Utah! and Mother Nature are
responsible for making Utah one of
the top winter tourist destinations in
the world. Ski Utah!, a marketing
and promotional subsidiary of the
Utah Ski Association, has effectively
gotten the word out to the world.*

*The association's brochures,
advertisements, and other
promotional campaigns highlight
the skiing possibilities in Utah. With
fourteen alpine ski resorts, and
what is described as the greatest
snow on earth, Utah is definitely a
skier's Eden. In 1993-1994, there
were 2.8 million skier days in Utah,
with a majority of those coming
from outside the state to feast on the
glorious snow and great ski terrain.*

Garbonzo Spicy Stew

Raelene Davis, marketing director, sends this recipe on behalf of
the entire Ski Utah! staff. Raelene has skied every Utah resort.
She says, "They're all great and I like each one for a different
reason. This stew can simmer in a crock pot all day while you
are out skiing Utah's famous white stuff."

1	pound hamburger
1	medium onion, chopped
1	tablespoon chili power, or to taste
2	garlic cloves, minced
	freshly ground pepper, to taste
1	15-ounce can garbanzo beans, drained
1	15-ounce can kidney beans, drained
1	15-ounce can pinto beans, drained
1	15-ounce can ranch-style beans
1	4-ounce can chopped green chiles
1	28-ounce can stewed tomatoes, do not drain
1	8-ounce can tomato sauce
1	16-ounce bottle salsa, or 2 cups homemade salsa
	grated Cheddar cheese for garnish

✸ To a skillet, add the hamburger, onion, chili powder, garlic
and ground black pepper and brown the hamburger until
it is no longer pink. Drain any fat from the meat.

✸ Combine all of the ingredients, including the browned-
meat mixture, in a crock pot and cook on low for 4-6
hours.

✸ Serve the chili with grated Cheddar cheese sprinkled on
top and a piece of your favorite corn bread. Serves 6-8.

jerry sloan

Jazz coach Jerry Sloan proves that nice guys sometimes finish first. Jerry is the winningest coach in the basketball team's history. He is also the fourth winningest coach among active NBA coaches. A quiet man off the court, Jerry brings out an intensity in his players that has earned two division titles. He knows hoops from the inside out. After an outstanding college basketball career, he played for the Chicago Bulls and was a two-time NBA All-Star player. Jerry and his wife, Bobbye, live in Salt Lake City with their three children.

Jazzy Blackberry Cobbler

For a brief two weeks in July, the Midwest produces delicious wild blackberries. No one can find or pick them faster than Coach Sloan. This is his favorite recipe.

Dough:

2⅓	cups Bisquick Original Baking Mix
½	cup milk
3	tablespoons sugar
3	tablespoons butter, at room temperature

Filling:

4	cups fresh blackberries
1	cup granulated sugar
2	tablespoons lemon juice
1	teaspoon corn starch
⅛	teaspoon salt
2	tablespoons butter
½	cup water

☀ Preheat oven to 425°.

☀ To prepare the dough: Combine the Bisquick, milk, sugar, and butter and mix well. Roll out ⅔ of the dough on a lightly-floured surface. Line the bottom of a 9x12-inch glass baking dish with the dough. Bake until light brown, about 15-20 minutes.

☀ To prepare the filling: Combine the blackberries, sugar, lemon juice, corn starch, salt, butter and water in a medium saucepan and simmer until thickened, about 5 minutes. Let cool.

☀ Remove Bisquick dough from oven, and pour the berry mixture over the bottom layer. Drop spoonfuls of the remaining dough on top of the berries and bake until golden, about 15 minutes. Serves 6-8.

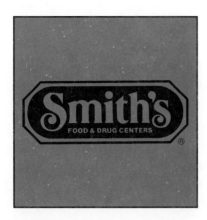

smith's
food & drug

Sixty years ago Smith's was a single, family owned-market in Brigham City. Today, there are 129 Smith's Food and Drug Centers in Arizona, California, Idaho, New Mexico, Nevada, Texas, Utah and Wyoming. Led by Chief Executive Officer Jeffrey Smith, the Salt Lake City-based corporation is a leading regional grocery and drug chain throughout eight Western States. Smith's carries on a proud tradition of the neighborhood American grocery store, while offering its customers a huge diversity of products in a contemporary atmosphere.

Smith's ABC Vegetable Soup for Kids

Shelley Thomas, vice president Public Affairs, submits this recipe. She says, "Smith's community commitment targets children through programs focusing on education, health, and nutrition. This recipe is low-fat, nutritious, and helps kids get their 5-A-Day, five servings of fruit and vegetables a day."

1	teaspoon Smith's vegetable oil
½	cup chopped onion
1	garlic clove, minced
2	14½-ounce cans Smith's chicken broth
1	15-ounce can crushed tomatoes
⅓	cup alphabet pasta
½	cup chopped parsley leaves
1	cup chopped broccoli
1	cup chopped carrots
1	cup sliced celery
	salt and pepper to taste
4	tablespoons Parmesan cheese

☀ Heat the oil in a large saucepan over medium heat. Add the onion and garlic, and sauté until onion is soft, about 2 minutes.

☀ Add the chicken broth, tomatoes, pasta, and parsley. Bring to a boil, reduce heat, and simmer for 10 minutes.

☀ Add the broccoli, carrots, and celery to the soup. Cook for an additional 10 minutes. Add salt and pepper to taste. Sprinkle the Parmesan cheese on top before serving. Serves 4-6 children.

The Stein Eriksen Lodge, nestled midmountain amidst the pristine aspens and spectacular scenery at Deer Valley Resort at Park City, is the ultimate get-away. With its old-world atmosphere, including Scandinavian furnishings, handpainted chandeliers from Italy, hand-crafted Portuguese tiles, and a total of 145 fireplaces, the Stein Eriksen Lodge represents the pinnacle of comfort and relaxed elegance. No wonder, **Condé Nast Traveler** *magazine named it the "Top Mainland Resort."*

Curried Coconut and Squash Soup with Roasted Corn and Lobster Fritters

This recipe is contributed by Executive Chef Mikel Trapp. It won first place in the Utah Chef's Soup and Sauce competition.

Curried Coconut and Squash Soup:

4	pounds butternut squash
2	medium onions
2	carrots, whole
1	tablespoon vegetable oil
2	tablespoons curry powder
	salt to taste
	white pepper to taste
1	16-ounce can coconut milk
1	48-ounce can chicken stock
2	cups sweet corn, cooked

Roasted Corn and Lobster Fritters:

½	cup all-purpose flour
½	teaspoon baking soda
½	teaspoon baking powder
½	cup buttermilk
2	egg yolks
¾	cup roasted corn
¾	cup lobster (or 6 ounces), steamed and cut into small dice (save the lobster stock)
2	egg whites
	salt to taste
	white pepper to taste
	olive oil or butter for frying
	minced chives and crème fraîche for garnish

To prepare the Curried Coconut and Squash Soup:

☀ Preheat oven to 375°.

☀ Cut the squash in half lengthwise, and discard the seeds. Set squash aside.

☀ Peel the onions and cut in half. Toss the carrots and onions lightly with vegetable oil. Place on baking sheet and roast for 20 minutes. Remove from oven, and cool.

☀ On the same baking sheet, roast the squash for 30 minutes. Cool.

108

Scrape the skin from the carrots, and cut carrots and onion into small dice.

Pour 1 tablespoon of vegetable oil into an 8-quart pot. Heat the oil over medium heat, and add the carrots, onions, curry powder, salt and pepper, and sauté for 2 minutes.

Add the coconut milk and chicken stock.

Scoop the flesh from the squash and add to the soup. Cook for 10 minutes.

Puree the soup and adjust seasonings to taste. Add cooked sweet corn. Heat the soup through, and keep warm.

To prepare the Roasted Corn and Lobster Fritters:

Sift the flour, baking soda, and baking powder into a mixing bowl. Add egg yolks, buttermilk, and 1 cup of the lobster stock. Mix well.

Beat the egg whites until stiff peaks form. Fold into batter.

Toss the roasted corn and lobster together. Fold the corn and lobster into the batter. Season with salt and white pepper.

Heat about 1 tablespoon of olive oil or butter in a deep skillet. Drop the fritter batter by the tablespoon into the hot oil. Fry, turning once, until golden, about 2-3 minutes. Do not crowd the skillet with batter. Drain the fritters on paper towels.

Ladle the soup into large bowls and place a fritter in the center of each bowl. Garnish with minced chives and crème fraîche. Serves 12.

martin stenger

Martin Stenger says that eating is one of his favorite pastimes. "I may have gotten this way from my lifestyle of bicycle racing, training and playing hard. I burn a lot of calories and boy can I eat, sometimes I really pack it in." If Martin's mountain bike racing achievements are an indication, he must have a very high food bill. He has been the Utah State Mountain Biking Champion seven times. He placed fifth in the 1989 World Championships, and he has eight years experience on the professional mountain bike circuit. Martin has lived in Utah twenty-two years and enjoys its awesome skiing and mountain bike riding, and an occasional antique bike race from one Salt Lake City bar to the next.

Izer's Famous Burnt Beans and Toast

"My most recent nick-name is 'Izer' and this recipe has a story behind it.

I was living in a house while attending school at the University of Utah and we named the place Buck Chub Boot Camp since we always had a few grommets, or rugrats running around, and/or junior racers from the Mid-West coming out to train with a pro from Utah. My roommate and good friend, Buck Chub, was always burning the beans and, well, it wasn't always, but if you have ever burned the beans good, or I mean bad, like real bad, then you know how foul the odor can be. Then we had this thing about toast. It seems like the toaster was always being used. Four bachelors in one house, we had to get two toasters, and one of them was a 4-banger. We were in toast heaven! It came with all sorts of clichés like, 'Everything eventually makes the transformation into toast.' It's true. Everything eventually breaks, or wears out, or gets tired. One of my roommates was always recalibrating the toasters. What does toast have to do with Mexican food? Simple: The toaster is just the best darn way to prepare your store-bought tortillas for eating. Just fold the tortilla in half, and toast. Set the toaster on light for flour, medium for corn. No oil, no hassle. Just don't burn the toast. Izer's Famous Burnt Beans and Toast is Mexican-food-lifestyle and a low-budget winner. Cook your own beans; tastier and healthier than canned beans, and if you do it right, no gas factor. If all else fails, follow the directions on the bean package."

1	cup black or pinto beans, dried, or 2 cups canned beans
2	teaspoons olive oil or canola oil
1	4-ounce can diced green chiles
2	garlic cloves, chopped fine
½	cup chopped white onion
1	teaspoon cumin seed (I prefer fresh ground—get the whole seeds and crush them yourself.)
½	teaspoon cayenne pepper
	salt to taste

☀ Soak the beans. Quick soak: In a large pan, add the beans and enough water to cover. Bring to a boil, put lid on, turn off heat and let sit for 1 hour. Or Slow soak: Soak the beans in water overnight. Or use canned beans.

☀ Drain and rinse the beans—the key to low-gas factor.

☀ To a stock pot, add the beans and cover liberally with

water. Turn the heat to high and boil, then cook on low heat until tender, about $1\frac{1}{2}$ hours. Don't over/undercook, or else......

☀ Drain and rinse the beans; the more, the merrier.

☀ At this point you can freeze excess beans. They only last 2-5 days in the fridge.

☀ In a cast-iron skillet, add the oil, and turn the heat to medium. Then, add the beans and all of the other ingredients and cook until beans have that refried, mushy texture.

☀ The beans are good with rice. Or over tortillas with grated, cheese, diced tomatoes, lettuce, salsa, chips, yogurt, avocado, or sour cream on top. Taco or Tostada-style. Or on the side. Serves 4.

Great White Throne

anne stirba

Anne Stirba is the fourth woman in Utah's history to preside over a district court. Appointed to the Third District Court in 1991 by Governor Norman Bangerter, Judge Stirba serves Salt Lake, Summit and Tooele counties. Before joining the bench, Anne was an assistant Utah attorney general and assistant United States attorney and was named Outstanding Young Lawyer of the Year in 1987 by the Utah State Bar. Anne and her husband, Peter, together with their two daughters, enjoy skiing, hiking, camping, fishing, golfing, horseback riding, and playing tennis.

You Be the Judge of My Salmon Pâté

The arresting flavors of salmon and horseradish are captured in this addictive and robust pâté. Serve it with your favorite crackers, bread, and green and red grapes.

2	cups cooked salmon
1	tablespoon Liquid Smoke
1	tablespoon horseradish
¼	cup mayonnaise
1	tablespoon lemon juice
4	ounces cream cheese, at room temperature
¼	teaspoon white pepper
1	tablespoon fresh chives, finely chopped
1	garlic clove, minced
	salt and pepper, to taste

☀ In a bowl, break the salmon apart into small flakes. Add the remaining ingredients and mix well.

☀ Spoon the salmon pâté into a colorful crock, and chill before serving. Makes 3 cups.

peggy stock

Peggy Stock is Utah's first female college president. She likes to describe herself quantitatively by starting with the number six. "One of my favorite hobbies is raising Arabian horses, and I have six of them. I have five children, three daughters and two sons. I have four careers. I've been an educator, a psychologist, a business consultant, and a CEO. I have three nonhuman loves in life: my great Dane, Hamlet; buying and restoring antique furniture; and frequently tasting sushi and sashimi. I have been the first woman president of two colleges: Colby-Sawyer College in New Hampshire, and now Westminster College in Salt Lake City. And I currently have one goal in life, making Westminster College the absolute best college it can possibly be. Barring that, my one goal in life would be to find the perfect fly-fishing spot and to go there with my husband Bob."

Molé Stew

The chocolate in this chili recipe is reminiscent of South-of-the-Border cuisine, while the spices hint of far-eastern fare. All blend into a fun meal for a get-together after a football game or a vigorous day hiking the trails outside of Salt Lake.

	kosher salt
1	pound ground beef chuck
1	medium onion, chopped
2	garlic cloves, minced
1	15-ounce can red kidney beans, rinsed and drained
1	cup barbecue sauce
¾	cup water
½	ounce bitter chocolate, grated
¼	cup tomato juice
¼	cup beer (optional)
½	teaspoon oregano
1	tablespoon chili powder
1	teaspoon black pepper
½	teaspoon ground cumin
½	teaspoon turmeric
½	teaspoon allspice
½	teaspoon cinnamon
¼	teaspoon ground cloves
¼	teaspoon ground coriander
¼	teaspoon ground cardamom
1	teaspoon salt
	grated cheese, chopped onions, sliced scallions, sour cream, or oyster crackers for garnish

❋ Sprinkle salt on a large skillet and heat for 30 seconds. Add the beef chuck, onion, and garlic and sauté until the meat is no longer pink, about 5-7 minutes. Drain, and transfer to a soup pot.

❋ Stir in red kidney beans, barbecue sauce, water, chocolate, tomato juice, optional beer, and herbs and spices, and bring to a boil. Reduce heat, and simmer 30 minutes. You may add more tomato sauce or beer if the mixture is too thick.

❋ Serve with grated cheese, chopped onions, sliced scallions, sour cream, or oyster crackers for garnish. Serves 4.

sundance institute

Lapin au Cidre et aux Pruneaux

Nicole Guillemet, vice president and general manager, submits this recipe for rabbit cooked in cider with prunes for the Sundance Institute.

3	cups cider
⅓	cup raisins
1	large rabbit, cut into 12 pieces
3	tablespoons unsalted butter, divided
1	tablespoon vegetable oil
1	cup Cognac or Brandy
1	cup shallots, finely chopped
3	garlic cloves, chopped
3	ounces bacon or pancetta
1 ½	tablespoons all-purpose flour
1 ½	cups chicken stock or white wine
1 ¼	cups dried prunes or apricots
	salt and freshly ground pepper, to taste
1	bay leaf
1	thyme sprig
1	parsley sprig

☀ Soak the raisins in the cider for 2 hours before preparing the rabbit. Drain, and reserve the cider. Set the raisins aside.

☀ Rinse the rabbit, and pat dry. Melt 2 tablespoons of the butter in a large, heavy-bottomed Dutch oven. Combine the vegetable oil with the melted butter. Add the rabbit, a few pieces at a time, and brown on all sides. Put all of the rabbit pieces in the Dutch oven, and add the Cognac Light the Cognac, and flambé for a few seconds. When the flame dies down, remove the rabbit, and drain on paper towels. Pour off the liquid and fat from the Dutch oven.

☀ Melt the remaining 1 tablespoon of butter in the Dutch oven. Add the shallots, garlic, and bacon. Cook over medium-low heat, stirring often. When the shallots begin to brown, add the flour, and whisk. Return the rabbit to the Dutch oven. Stir in the cider, chicken stock, and herbs. Add the salt and freshly ground pepper, to taste. Bring to a boil, and cook on high for 10 minutes. Reduce heat to low. Cover and simmer for 45 minutes, or until the rabbit easily falls away from the bones. Stir every so often.

114 ☀

Add the prunes and raisins, and simmer for an additional
5 minutes. Taste for seasoning. Serve with rice, potatoes,
or pasta. Serves 6.

Bryce Canyon National Park, Panel 1

mike taggett

Mike Taggett seized an idea, turned it into a product, and with unfailing enthusiasm he has created Chums, a thriving and profitable business. While working as a river guide on the Colorado River, Mike saw clients lose pair after pair of valuable eyeglasses. So in 1983, he bought a sewing machine, taught himself to sew and began designing and making functional eyeglass retainers. An early prototype, called JERCS, or Just An Eyeglass Retention and Comfort System, had design faults. Mike improved the design so that the retainer firmly connected to the eyeglasses and held them securely around the head and began manufacturing the next generation's product, Chums. While the first years were rocky, Mike's faith in his product was never shaken. Now Chums come in several different styles and Mike has expanded into sportswear clothing, a line he calls HelloWear. Recently, Chums, located in Hurricane, Utah, shipped its ten millionth Original Chum.

Chef Mason's Rock Shrimp Cakes

When Mike is home in Hurricane, Utah, he's too busy to do much cooking. But, when Mike is on the road, selling Chums all over the world, he is a connoisseur of fine food. One of Mike's favorite recipes on the face of the earth is Rock Shrimp Cakes from the Ketchum Grill in Ketchum, Idaho.

2	teaspoons unsalted butter
1	medium onion, minced fine
1	stalk celery, minced fine
¼	teaspoon Tabasco sauce
⅓	teaspoon white pepper, ground
2	teaspoons fresh dill, chopped fine
1	dash kosher salt
2	8-ounce packages of cream cheese, at room temperature
2	egg yolks
6	ounces rock shrimp, peeled, rinsed, drained, and coarsely chopped
1⅓	cups Japanese-style bread crumbs (found in specialty food stores), divided
2	teaspoons olive oil

☀ Melt the butter in a sauté pan, and sauté onion and celery until translucent. Add Tabasco sauce, white pepper, fresh dill, and salt. Mix together and set aside.

☀ In a mixer equipped with a paddle, cream together the cream cheese and egg yolks in a large mixing bowl. Stir in the onion and celery mixture. Add the rock shrimp and stir well. Reserve ½ cup of the bread crumbs, and mix in the remaining bread crumbs to help bind the cheese mixture. Chill in refrigerator for at least 30 minutes, or up to 2-3 days if preparing the batter ahead.

☀ Form the shrimp mixture into ½-inch thick silver dollar-sized cakes. Pat remaining bread crumbs on each side of the cakes to keep them from sticking in the pan.

☀ To a pre-heated sauté pan, add olive oil. Brown the shrimp cakes on one side, about 3-4 minutes, flip, reduce heat, and cook until heated through, about 5 minutes. Do not crowd the cakes in the pan, or they will be hard to flip. The cakes can be held in a warm oven while the others are cooking.

☀ Serve cakes with your favorite rémoulade, tartar or aïoli sauce. Serves 8.

hamilton teichert

116

Hamilton Teichert isn't one of those cowboy poets who draws his words from shoot-'em-up movies or the daydreams of a would-be cowboy. Hamilton's verse comes right from the heart and the saddle. His is the voice of experience. He grew up a Hereford cattle ranch in Cokeville, Wyoming and has spent the majority of his adult life as a cattle rancher. After twenty-five years of ranching, Hamilton thought he'd retire from cowboy life and he and his wife, Shirley, headed for the warmer climate of St. George. But life hasn't slowed down a bit. Hamilton is constantly in demand and performs his cowboy poetry shows with trick horses and ropes throughout the West. The Teicherts spend each summer at Ruby's Inn near Bryce Canyon National Park.

Broncobuster Caramel Corn

If'n you don't have a milk cow clothed in silk
Then use one can of Eagle Brand Milk.

Next to help the old bugger
Add one package of brown sugar.

Now cowboy as you step down out of your stirrup
Add one can of Karo Syrup.

In this recipe you don't need gin
but you do need one square of margarine.

A few more things you should know
Combine these ingredients and cook on low.

Stir slow and quite often
So this ball will soften.

Pour it over freshly popped corn
And you'll have four gallons of Caramel Corn.

kristi terzian

Kristi Terzian moved to Utah twelve years ago to ski at the famous Rowmark Ski Academy. With the expertise she gained there and an abundance of natural talent, she became a member of the U.S. Alpine Ski Team and a U.S. National Champion in 1990, 1993, and 1994. She set American records in 1990 and 1991 for the most top fifteen finishes in a single World Cup season. A junior at the University of Utah, Kristi is studying German and business. She established Primo's Espresso Americana at the Park City Resort and is an ambassador of skiing for the Park City Ski Area. When ski season is over, Kristi lugs out her camping gear and mountain bike for enjoyable trips to the Uinta Mountains or Moab.

Black Diamond Pizza

Crust:

1	package (1 tablespoon) active yeast
1	cup warm water
1	tablespoon honey
1½	cups whole wheat flour
1¼	cups all-purpose flour

Topping:

2	chicken breasts, boneless, skinless, cut into bite-size pieces
2	tablespoons soy sauce
4	garlic cloves, minced
½	cup brown sugar
1	cup rice vinegar
½	cup soy sauce
4	tablespoons peanut butter
6	tablespoons water
2	teaspoons minced fresh ginger
1-2	teaspoons red pepper flakes
6	ounces Mozzarella cheese, grated
	chopped fresh cilantro, for topping

☀ To prepare the crust: In a large bowl, dissolve the yeast in the warm water, and add the honey. Let stand for 5 minutes. Gradually add the whole wheat flour and all-purpose flour, and work the ingredients together until the dough holds its shape. Turn the dough onto a lightly floured surface, and knead until smooth and elastic. Place dough in a lightly-oiled bowl, cover, and place in a warm place for about 1 hour, or until the dough doubles in size.

☀ Preheat oven to 500°. Lightly oil a baking sheet or pizza pan.

☀ To prepare the topping: Coat a sauté pan with non-stick cooking spray, and sauté the chicken with 2 tablespoons soy sauce and the garlic for 3 minutes, or until the chicken is no longer pink.

☀ In a large skillet, combine the brown sugar, rice vinegar, soy sauce, peanut butter, water, ginger, and red pepper flakes. Bring to a boil, and simmer for 5-7 minutes until thickened. You may further thicken with cornstarch, or add water, if necessary. Stir in the chicken mixture.

118

To assemble the pizza: Roll the dough out on a flat surface and form into a circle. Place the dough on the baking sheet or pizza pan. Sprinkle 2 ounces cheese over the dough, top with chicken/peanut butter mixture, and spread the rest of the cheese on top.

Bake 10 minutes until edges are brown. Reduce heat to 350° and cook for 10-15 minutes. You may top with chopped fresh cilantro. Serves 4.

al unser

Al Unser belongs among the pantheon of racing greats. He is one of only four drivers to win two consecutive Indy 500s (1970 and 1971). A true racing legend who at the age of eighteen began his career racing a modified Roadster, Al has many victories to his name. A four-time Indy 500 winner, three-time Indy Car World Series Champion, inductee into the Motorsports Hall of Fame, and two-time Pikes Peak Hill Climb Winner are just some of the many accomplishments Al has achieved as a racing champion. And the Unser legacy continues on as Al remains a strong competitor and challenges his son Al Unser Jr., winner of the 1992 Indy 500. The third generation is coming up close behind with Al Jr.'s son Albert, who at the age of ten, began racing go-karts. The Unsers slow down the pace at Lake Powell, where tooling around the lake provides immeasurable pleasure.

Mom Unser's "Indy" Chili

1	pound lean pork (tenderloin, chops, or ground)
1	medium onion, chopped
1	garlic clove, minced
1	28-ounce can tomatoes
1	shake oregano
	salt to taste
3	4-ounce cans green chiles
1	15-ounce can pinto beans, drained (optional)

☀ If using tenderloin or chops, remove the fat from the pork, and cut into 1-inch cubes.

☀ In a large skillet, sauté the pork, onion, and garlic over medium heat until the pork is browned, about 5-7 minutes.

☀ Squeeze the tomatoes through your fingers to break-up, and add to the skillet with the tomato juice. Add oregano and salt, to taste. Add the green chiles and the optional pinto beans, and simmer for 35 minutes. Add water if too thick. Serves 4.

robert & heather urich

They are both Toronto natives whose talents brought them to the States and finally to a chance encounter. Robert Urich came to Florida on a football scholarship. Heather Menzies played Louisa, the second-eldest von Trapp daughter in the classic **Sound of Music.** *As fate would have it, they met while filming a commercial for Libby's Corned Beef Hash. Robert became an Emmy-winning actor and the star of ten television series, including* **Vegas,** *and most recently,* **The Lazarus Man** *from Castle Rock Entertainment/Turner Program Series. When not before the cameras, Bob is active in natural resource conservation and publishes a series of outdoor books under the banner, Beaver Dam Press. Heather is active in community affairs and a board member of the Park City Performing Arts Center. The Urichs live in Deer Valley.*

Bob's Kabobs

Heather says, "You can choose other vegies and herbs for Bob's Kabobs. Rosemary is great, and mushrooms are terrific."

1	pound chicken, boneless and skinless, cut into 1-inch cubes
8	cherry tomatoes
8	pearl onions
$\frac{1}{2}$	green bell pepper, cut into 1-inch pieces
$\frac{1}{2}$	red bell pepper, cut into 1-inch pieces

Marinade:

1	garlic clove, minced
2	tablespoons balsamic vinegar
6	tablespoons olive oil
1	tablespoon freshly squeezed lemon juice (optional)
	salt and pepper, to taste
	fresh thyme sprigs, for garnish

☀ In a large bowl, combine the chicken, tomatoes, pearl onions, and green and red peppers.

☀ To prepare the marinade: In a small bowl, combine the garlic, balsamic vinegar, olive oil, and lemon juice. Stir in salt and pepper to taste.

☀ Pour the marinade over the chicken and vegetables. Toss to coat. Lightly cover, and marinate for at least one hour.

☀ Prepare the charcoals for grilling.

☀ Thread the chicken and vegetables onto skewers.

☀ Grill for 7-8 minutes, turning frequently, until lightly browned.

☀ Arrange the kabobs on a platter, and garnish with fresh thyme sprigs. Serve with rice or risotto, and a fresh green salad. Serves 2-4.

Utah Opera has established itself as one of the leading regional opera companies in North American with its distinctive productions from the classical repertoire and its many contributions to the modern development of the art form. Three productions each season, featuring the finest in national and international artists, are presented in Salt Lake City's stately Capitol Theatre. Productions are frequently sold out before their run indicating the popularity of opera along the Wasatch Front. All operas are sung in their original language with English translations provided by Supertitles on an overhead screen.

Utah Opera Fudge Cake

This recipe was sent compliments of Darleen Merrihew and is the treat of choice whenever there is a celebration at the Utah Opera Company office.

Fudge Cake:

2	sticks (1 cup) margarine
4	tablespoons cocoa
1	cup water
2	cups all-purpose flour
½	teaspoon salt
2	cups granulated sugar
2	eggs
½	cup milk
1	teaspoon vanilla extract
½	teaspoon baking soda

Frosting:

1	stick (½ cup) margarine
4	tablespoons cocoa
1	teaspoon vanilla extract
½	cup milk
	dash of salt
4	cups powdered sugar
1	cup chopped nuts

☀ Preheat oven to 375°. Grease and flour a 12x9-inch pan.

☀ To prepare the fudge cake: In a saucepan, bring to a boil the margarine, cocoa, and water. Stir constantly until margarine is melted and the cocoa mixed in. Set aside. In a mixing bowl, stir together the flour, salt, and sugar. Pour the hot margarine mixture into the flour mixture with the beaters going. Add the eggs, milk, soda, and vanilla extract and mix well. Pour the batter into the prepared pan, and bake for 30 minutes. Remove from oven and let cool at least 5 minutes.

☀ To prepare the frosting: In a saucepan, melt the margarine, and add the cocoa, vanilla, milk, and a dash of salt. Bring the mixture to a boil for a few minutes, stirring constantly. Remove from heat. Place the powdered sugar in a mixing bowl. Pour in the hot cocoa mixture with the beaters going and blend well. Gently fold in the chopped nuts. Spread the frosting over the cake. Serves 12-14.

raymond van mason

122

Raymond Van Mason began his training under Tamara Gladikova in Salt Lake City and the University of Utah, receiving a bachelor's degree of fine arts in ballet. He joined Ballet West in 1983, was promoted to soloist in 1987, and became a principal artist in 1989. With Ballet West, one of the nation's leading performing arts organizations, he has performed the principal roles in **Swan Lake, Giselle, Sleeping Beauty, The Nutcracker,** *and many others. Raymond is also a talented choreographer and has choreographed several works for Ballet West, including* **Chameleon** *and* **Carmina Burana,** *and the world premiere of his* **Symphony #7.**

Chocolate Zucchini Banana Bread

3	cups all-purpose flour
1	teaspoon salt
1	teaspoon baking soda
¼	teaspoon baking powder
½	teaspoon cloves
½	teaspoon nutmeg
3	teaspoons cinnamon
1	cup granulated sugar
1	cup brown sugar
3	eggs, beaten
1	cup oil
2	cups grated zucchini
3	teaspoons vanilla extract
4	over-ripe bananas, mashed
1	package See's chocolate chips
1	cup walnuts, chopped (optional)

☀ Preheat oven to 325°. Butter three 9x5x3-inch loaf pans.

☀ In a mixing bowl, combine the flour, salt, baking soda, baking powder, cloves, nutmeg, and cinnamon.

☀ In another larger mixing bowl, cream together the granulated sugar, brown sugar, eggs, and oil. Stir in the grated zucchini, vanilla, mashed bananas, chocolate chips, and optional walnuts.

☀ To the wet ingredients, gradually stir in the dry ingredients, and mix until just blended. Do not over mix.

☀ Pour the batter into the prepared loaf pans, and bake until a knife or skewer inserted in the middle of the loaf comes out clean, about 60 minutes. Makes 3 loaves.

wasatch beers

Greg Schirf began a modern-day brewing tradition in 1986, when he began blending malted barley and roasted hops at Utah's first microbrewery. Today, the award-winning brewery, located in Park City's historic downtown district, is known throughout the West for producing such favorites as Slickrock Lager, Weizenbier, and Wasatch Premium Ale. With careful attention to quality, Wasatch Beers has increased production each year, fortunately, considering the Pub's slogan, "We drink our share and sell the rest." The brew pub's atmosphere is casual and unassuming and the fare delightful.

Wasatch Beer Bread

¼	cup active dry yeast
¾	cup warm water
3	cups Wasatch Wheat Beer
	dash of salt
¾	cup vegetable shortening
⅛	cup caraway seeds
¾	cup molasses
9-11	cups all-purpose flour

☀ In a bowl, add the yeast to the warm water, and stir to combine. Let the mixture sit until the yeast begins to foam and grow. Meanwhile, warm the beer in a saucepan.

☀ In a large mixing bowl, combine the yeast mixture with the warmed beer. Add the salt, shortening, caraway seeds, and molasses. Mix thoroughly.

☀ Gradually add the flour to the yeast-molasses mixture until the dough forms a mass and is completely removed from the sides of the bowl.

☀ Cover the bowl, and set in a warm place. Let the dough rise for 25-30 minutes.

☀ Preheat oven to 350°. Butter or oil six 9x5x3-inch loaf pans.

☀ Punch down the dough. Cut and divide the dough into 6 equal portions. Knead each portion on a lightly floured surface until the dough is smooth and elastic.

☀ Place the dough portions in the prepared loaf pans. Place the loaf pans in a warm place, and allow dough to rise for an additional 45 minutes.

☀ Bake until the bread is a deep golden brown, about 25-30 minutes. Cool on a wire rack. Makes 6 loaves.

wasatch fault

The Wasatch Fault is definitely one of the biggest movers and shakers in Utah. A fault is a fracture in which one section of the Earth's crust has been displaced. Eighty percent of Utah's residents live along this quake-prone zone. The Wasatch Range was formed along the Wasatch Fault line as a result of the fault's long-term, cumulative upward displacement of thousands of meters of rock. A recent study of the fault, compiling a 6,000-year history of major Wasatch earthquakes, indicates that only one of the fault's segments has not generated a quake during the last 1,400 years. Researchers have identified a fault segment, near Brigham City, as the only one with notable risk of producing a shock in the foreseeable future. They calculate a seven to fifteen percent chance the segment will produce a magnitude seven or larger earthquake in the next century.

Tasty Quake

If you'd like to teach your children about earthquakes, try this simple recipe.

During an earthquake, layers of rock under the soil break apart suddenly and energy is released in the form of waves. You can simulate this release of energy by watching what happens to a pan of gelatin.

This recipe has been carefully tested: To transmit waves that can be seen easily, the pan must be metal, and it must be full nearly to the top with the gelatin mixture. Tasty Quake is sent compliments of the University of Utah Seismograph Station.

2	6-ounce packages of red or purple gelatin dessert
2	1-serving envelopes of unflavored gelatin
4	cups boiling water
4	cups cold water

☀ Empty the gelatin dessert and unflavored gelatin into a 12x9-inch metal baking pan. Add the boiling water, and stir until all of the powder is dissolved. Add the cold water, and stir to mix. Chill in refrigerator for at least 3 hours, or until set.

☀ Gently tap the side of the pan of gelatin, while holding the pan firmly with the other hand. Kids should be able to see the waves traveling through the gelatin. Compare the gelatin to the ground, the tap of your hand to the rocks breaking, and the waves in the gelatin to earthquake waves. Serves 10.

tom watkins

*Tom Watkins journal of photographs and words, **Stone Time**, is his personal testament to "the home of my heart," the place where "stone and sky and water speak the language of memory." The place is the wildland region of southern Utah, through which Tom has trekked with notebook and camera. The pictures, in black and white, are stark and stunning. The words, as always with Tom, flow with power and urgency. Royalties from the sale of the book have been given to The Wilderness Society, which one day hopes to make this home of the heart a designated wilderness area. Tom is editor of **Wilderness**, the quarterly magazine of The Wilderness Society. He is also a vice president of the Society.*

Wild as Utah Pork Chop Casserole

4	loin pork chops, about 1-inch thick
1	tablespoon unsalted butter
2	large apples
1	medium onion, coarsely chopped
¾	teaspoon cinnamon

☀ Preheat oven to 350°.

☀ In a large skillet, melt the butter, and brown the pork chops over medium-high heat, about 2 minutes per side. Remove the chops, and cut them, removing the bone, into 8 pieces of equal size.

☀ Peel and core the apples, and cut into horizontal slices.

☀ In a 3-quart casserole dish, place 2 pieces of the pork chops on the bottom, and cover with ¼ of the apple slices. Sprinkle lightly with cinnamon, and spread ¼ of the onions on top of the apples.

☀ Continue layering until the ingredients are gone.

☀ Bake for 45 minutes. Add water, if needed, to keep chops moist. Serves 4.

126

tom welch

He's the man who will bring the world to Salt Lake City. Since 1985, Tom Welch has headed the bid committee dedicated to winning the 2002 Olympics for Utah. But, the Olympic quest has not been without personal sacrifice. Tom endured defeat at the hands of other city contenders, traveled almost non-stop, missing his son's rugby championship game and daughter's high school graduation, and quit his high paying job for this volunteer position. When the International Olympic Committee pronounced in 1995 that Salt Lake City had been awarded the Games—and a crowd of 40,000 people who had gathered in downtown Salt Lake to watch the broadcast live on an enormous television screen cheered exuberantly—Tom must have felt that it was all worth it.

Hunter's Dessert

Hasty Pudding:

2	tablespoons butter
2	cups boiling water
1	cup brown sugar
1	teaspoon butter
½	cup granulated sugar
½	cup milk or apple cider
1	cup flour
½	teaspoon baking soda
½	teaspoon salt
½	teaspoon cinnamon
½	cup raisins
½	cup chopped nuts
2	apples, peeled and diced

Apple Cider Sauce:

½	cup packed brown sugar
¼	cup butter
¼	cup apple cider
2	tablespoons whipping cream

☀ Preheat oven to 350°.

☀ To prepare Hasty Pudding: Put 2 tablespoons butter into a mixing bowl. Pour the boiling water over the butter to melt. Add the brown sugar, and stir until it is dissolved. Set aside.

☀ In a mixing bowl, cream together 1 teaspoon butter and granulated sugar. Stir in the milk or apple cider.

☀ In a separate bowl, combine the flour, baking soda, salt, and cinnamon.

☀ Add the dry ingredients to the creamed butter and sugar mixture. Fold in the raisins, chopped nuts, and apples.

☀ Spread the raisin and apple mixture onto the bottom of a 8x8x2-inch baking pan. Pour the dissolved butter-water mixture over it.

☀ Bake for 30-35 minutes. Chill before serving.

☀ To prepare Apple Cider Sauce: Add the sauce ingredients to a pan, and stirring continuously, boil for 3 minutes. Do not burn.

☀ Serve the Hasty Pudding topped with the Apple Cider Sauce and whipped cream. Serves 6-8.

don weller

*Don Weller has created illustrations and designs that have won the most coveted awards in his profession. Those art pieces have also brought style and charm to our lives. He has designed and illustrated countless artwork, logos, symbols, and publications for clients around the world, including INTEL, Alaska Airlines, the Tournament of Roses, the U.S. Postal Service, and the National Football League. He has published three books, **Park City, Seashells and Sunsets**, and, most recently, **The Cutting Horse**. Don, his wife, Cha Cha, and his firm, The Weller Institute for the Cure of Design, moved from Los Angeles to Oakley in 1984. Don says he loves Utah's snow and classifies himself as a "terminally intermediate skier with delusions of grandeur."*

Gyoza

"My wife Cha Cha makes this irresistible recipe for Japanese wontons. This adaptation of Chinese dimsums are called gyoza in Japanese."

Stuffing or Gu:

1	package Dynasty bean threads or saifun
2	chicken breasts, skinned, boned, and chopped into 2-inch pieces
1	small head Chinese or Napa cabbage, chopped into 1-inch pieces
2	bunches green onion, chopped very fine
3	garlic cloves, minced
1	carrot, peeled and grated
2	packages wonton skins, or gyoza/pot sticker skins
	sesame oil

Dipping Sauce:

3	tablespoons soy sauce
3	tablespoons rice vinegar
1-2	drops of chili oil, or la yu

✺ To prepare the bean threads or saifun: Boil 4 cups of water, and pour over the bean thread noodles. Soak for 5-10 minutes until soft. Drain.

✺ To prepare the stuffing or gu: Put the chicken, cabbage, and bean threads in the food processor and mince until a smooth, pasty consistency. Put the processed chicken mixture into a large mixing bowl. Add the green onion, garlic, and grated carrots, and mix well by hand. Now the gu is ready.

✺ To prepare the wontons or gyoza: Place a wonton skin on a flat surface. Put a small amount of the stuffing or gu just below the center of the wonton skin. Dip your fingers in water and lightly wet the edges of the dough. Fold one corner of the wonton skin over the stuffing to make a triangle, and pinch the edges together to seal. Repeat until stuffing is gone.

✺ You will probably have to fry and steam the wontons in batches. Heat a large frying pan over medium heat or get out your electric skillet. Pour 1-2 tablespoons sesame oil in the bottom of the pan and swirl to coat the bottom evenly. When oil is nice and hot, place the wontons, flat-side down, in the skillet. Cook 2-3 minutes to brown the bottom of the wontons. Pour 1 cup of water over the wontons, cover tightly, and steam for 3-5 minutes. Do not peek or open the lid for at least the first 2 minutes.

128 ☀

Repeat, replenishing the sesame oil as needed.

To prepare the dipping sauce: In a small bowl, mix the soy sauce, rice vinegar, and chili oil. The chili oil isn't as hot as you remember. Now you are ready to dip the gyoza. Serves 4.

Temples and Towers of the Virgin

fred wix

*Fred Wix started his career as a gourmet cook at an early age. At five years old, Fred was roasting just-reeled-in fish over an open fire. With those humble beginnings, Fred is now one of the nation's most popular chefs. His program, **Gabby Gourmet**, is seen five days a week throughout the West. He has traveled around the world, seeking out new tastes and flavors, and showing off his kitchen magic. He conducts cooking classes in his cooking school at ZCMI in Salt Lake City and also takes his classes on the road to gourmets-in-training across the country. Fred settled in Salt Lake City to raise his two daughters after retiring from the Marine Corps.*

Gabby's Own Mustard

Homemade mustard can be prepared from crushed mustard seeds or mustard powder. If using mustard seeds, just soak the seeds overnight, and crush them in a mortar and pestle, and proceed with the recipe as usual. Homemade mustard is a unique gift for your gourmet-inclined friends. The Gabby Gourmet suggests "pouring the mustard into a decorative jar or crock with a ribbon around the lid, and a copy of the recipe attached. They will love you for it, and best of all, it's really simple to make."

½	cup all-purpose flour
¼	cup granulated sugar
½	cup dry mustard
¾	cup cider vinegar
⅛	teaspoon salt

☀ In a mixing bowl, blend all the ingredients together until smooth. Pour the mixture into a crock or old "mayo" and cover tightly.

☀ Refrigerate the mixture for 7 (count 'em, Seven) days. Every couple of days, shake the jar a couple of seconds. After 7 days, stir and serve as you would any prepared mustard, oh, maybe just not as much. In fact, definitely not as much. Makes 1 pint.

trace worthington

Trace "The Ace" Worthington performs some aerial acrobatics typical of an ace pilot. But, the machine he pilots is his body, propelled high in the air in freestyle aerial ski jumping. A three-time Overall World Cup Champion, and World Aerial Champion, Trace is the only person in the world to consistently perform a quadruple twisting somersault and he is the first double gold medal winner in the history of the World Freestyle Ski Championships. A native of Minnesota, Trace now lives in Park City and practices at the Bear Hollow Olympic Jump Complex. He says Utah provides the perfect environment for an athlete to train for an Olympic gold medal, a goal Trace will certainly achieve.

D'Aurelio & Sons Olive and Angel Hair Pasta

"My roommate's Uncle Jim, owner of D'Aurelio & Sons Italian Restaurant, came to visit for a couple of weeks. Jim made a few of his best pasta dishes, and this was my favorite. If you are too lazy to cook, like me, make a huge pot of this pasta sauce for leftovers. Or better yet, don't cook at all, go to D'Aurelio & Sons in Park City, and request this entrée."

⅓	cup olive oil
1	cup pitted imported black olives, chopped
1	green bell pepper, cut into julienne
1	red bell pepper, cut into julienne
1	small red onion, chopped
4-6	garlic cloves, minced
	salt and freshly ground pepper, to taste
2	tablespoons slivered fresh basil
4	tablespoons chopped fresh parsley
	fresh Parmesan cheese, grated
1	pound angel hair pasta

☀ Set the oven at 225°, and place a pasta bowl in the oven to warm.

☀ Place a large sauté pan over medium heat, and add the olive oil when the pan is hot. Add the black olives, green bell pepper, red bell pepper, and red onion, and sauté for 6-7 minutes.

☀ Push the olive and vegetable mixture to the outside of the sauté pan, forming a circle. Add garlic to the middle of the pan, and sauté for about 2 minutes, but don't brown. Now, stir all of the ingredients together, adding the salt and freshly ground pepper, to taste. Keep warm.

☀ Meanwhile, bring a large pot of water to a boil. Add the angel hair pasta, and a splash of olive oil. Cook at a rolling boil for 2-3 minutes. Drain.

☀ Pour the pasta noodles into the warmed pasta bowl. Stir in the olive and vegetable mixture. Top with fresh basil, parsley, and Parmesan. Serves 4.

charmian wright

Veterinarian Charmian Wright and her husband, pilot Gordon Croissant, own and operate the only commercial camel-trekking business in the United States. After taking a camel expedition through Australia, Charmian and Gordon decided to try the venture, and, in 1991, the Park City couple bought a dromedary named Liza. Now, they have nine camels, including Liza's baby. Camels are sure-footed, friendly, intelligent, powerful, and, Charmian says, they are not smelly, contrary to popular opinion. Charmian leads the camels on occasional treks into such remote places as the San Rafael Swell, a desert region in the central part of state.

Camel Milk Biscuits

If camel's milk is not available, substitute cow, goat, sheep, or mare's milk, and add ¼ teaspoon salt. This recipe is for Dutch-oven outdoor style dining, but you can make the biscuits at home, too. Bake in an oven at 450° for 12-15 minutes.

480	milliliters all-purpose flour, sifted, or 2 cups
15	milliliters baking powder, or 1 tablespoon
60	milliliters butter, or 4 tablespoons
180	milliliters warm camel's milk, or ¾ cup

☀ Prepare 25 charcoals so they are lightly gray when you are ready to cook the biscuits.

☀ In a medium-size bowl, combine the sifted flour and baking powder (and salt if substituting the camel's milk.) Cut the butter into the flour mixture with a fork until it resembles the consistency of coarse corn meal.

☀ Stir the milk into the dry ingredients until the mixture forms a soft dough.

☀ Knead dough lightly on a floured surface for about 30 seconds. Roll the dough out to 1 centimeter (or ¼ inch) thickness. Using the top of your camp cup, cut the dough into rounds.

☀ Lightly grease the bottom of a Dutch oven. Arrange the biscuits about ½-inch apart on the bottom of the Dutch oven. Place 8-10 charcoals on the ground, and set the Dutch oven on top. Cover the Dutch oven, and place 12-15 coals on the lid. Bake at 232°C (or 450°F) for 12-15 minutes. Serve with wild honey. Makes 8 biscuits.

maggie wright

Maggie Wright is the ideal of grace and beauty on stage as Ballet West's principal female artist. She is noted for her portrayals of Anna in Andre Prokovsky's **Anna Karenina**, *Olympe in Val Caniparoli's* **Lady of the Camellias**, *and the title role in Ben Stevenson's* **Cinderella**. *On stage it appears as though gravitational forces have been suspended, but there is also an earthy side to this prima ballerina. Maggie loves gardening, working on her house, and relaxing with her husband, Dennis Tesch, and their three cats. She also attends classes at the University of Utah, where she is working toward a degree in physical therapy.*

Spinach Madeline

This is one of those magical dishes in that the flavor improves if it is made ahead and refrigerated overnight. It may also be frozen.

2	packages frozen spinach
4	tablespoons butter
2	tablespoons all-purpose flour
2	tablespoons chopped onion
½	cup evaporated milk
½	cup vegetable stock
½	teaspoon black pepper
¾	teaspoon celery salt
¾	teaspoon garlic salt
	salt, to taste
1	teaspoon Worcestershire sauce
	cayenne pepper, to taste (optional)
6	ounces jalapeño cheese, cut into cubes
	bread crumbs

☀ Cook spinach according to the directions on the label. Drain.

☀ Melt the butter in a saucepan over low heat, add the flour, and stir until blended and smooth, but not brown. Add the onion and cook until soft, but not brown. Add the evaporated milk and vegetable stock, stirring constantly to avoid lumps, and cook until smooth and thick. Add the black pepper, celery salt, garlic salt, salt, Worcestershire sauce, optional cayenne pepper, and cheese, and stir until cheese is melted.

☀ Add the spinach to the cheese mixture and stir until warm. Transfer to a warmed serving dish, top with bread crumbs and serve.

☀ If prepared the night before, simply reheat in a 350° oven for 30 minutes. Serves 8.

steve young

So why is Steve Young so often described as Utah's most eligible bachelor? Never mind that the San Francisco 49ers' quarterback won the Super Bowl MVP Award. Never mind that the articulate football player, who holds a juris doctorate degree from Brigham Young University, is sought out by prestigious firms like Nike and **Forbes** *magazine to endorse their products. Or that at 34 years old, Steve has the strength and abdominals of a 20-year-old. Or that the blue-eyed Young is tall, dark and, yes, handsome. Beyond all those things (which most women care very little about), is one "nice guy." He set up a charity called the Forever Young Foundation; he tithes regularly and has taught Sunday school classes. A native of Salt Lake City, Steve loves his home state for its friendly people, clean air, and great skiing. Steve, the feeling is mutual.*

Mom's Chocolate Chip Cookies

For the really brave, Steve suggests his Cookie Sandwich. "Take two hot, just out-of-the-oven cookies and put raw dough between them," he says. "Yummy."

4	cups all-purpose flour
¾	cup quick rolled oats
2	teaspoons baking soda
2	teaspoons salt
2	cups Crisco shortening
1½	cups granulated sugar
1½	cups brown sugar, packed
2	teaspoons vanilla extract
4	large eggs
4	cups Nestle Toll House chocolate morsels
	nuts, optional

☀ Preheat oven to 375°.

☀ Stir the flour, rolled oats, baking soda, and salt together in a mixing bowl.

☀ In a larger mixing bowl, beat together the shortening, granulated sugar, brown sugar, and vanilla. Add the eggs, one at a time, and mix thoroughly. Gradually add the flour mixture, beating until smooth. Stir in the chocolate morsels and nuts.

☀ Drop the dough by rounded tablespoons onto ungreased baking sheets. Bake for 9-11 minutes, or until golden brown. Remove from oven and let sit for a few minutes before transferring to wire racks to cool. Makes 10 dozen, or enough for a football team.

134

With its sheer cliffs and monoliths that reach high into the heavens, Zion National Park spreads across 147,000 acres and contains eight geologic formations and four major vegetation zones within elevations ranging from 3,666 to 8,726 feet. The Zion Lodge sits at the heart of the park and very near the Great White Throne and other park landmarks. The original Zion Lodge burned to the ground in 1965. A new lodge was built on the original foundation, and, in 1990, that lodge was remodeled to look like the original structure. The interior's light pine paneling adds warmth to the rustic rock and log lodge. Visitors enjoy a varied menu that includes family and gourmet dining, and the dining area opens to a large terrace.

Chicken Vera Cruz

4	pounds chicken breasts, boned and skinned

Jerk Paste:

½	cup Caribbean jerk spice
½	cup olive oil
½	cup balsamic vinegar
¼	cup sliced green onions

Red Onion Relish:

4	tablespoons butter, clarified
2	pounds red onions, chopped thin
½	pound red cabbage, shredded
1	cup brown sugar, packed
¾	cup red wine or Burgundy wine
¾	cup red wine vinegar
½	cup sweet red pepper, diced small

✻ Place the chicken breasts on a flat surface and pound thin to tenderize.

✻ To prepare the Jerk Paste: Combine all ingredients and blend thoroughly.

✻ Rub the paste over the chicken and marinate in the refrigerator for 4 hours.

✻ To prepare the Red Onion Relish: In a large sauté pan, melt the butter and sauté the onion and cabbage over medium heat until onions are translucent and begin to caramelize slightly. Add the brown sugar and quickly blend into the onion mix. Immediately add the wine and vinegar. Simmer and reduce until all the liquid is absorbed and evaporated. Add the red bell pepper, and continue cooking another 10 minutes, until mixture is dark reddish-purple in color. Remove from heat and refrigerate in a non-reactive container. Serve chilled.

✻ Prepare the coals for grilling.

✻ Cook the marinated chicken on the charcoal grill or broil for 2½-3 minutes per side, or until cooked through.

✻ Transfer the chicken to a serving platter and top with the chilled Red Onion Relish. Serves 8.

about the artist

Like the natural scenes he paints, Anton "Tony" Rasmussen continuously changes his painting style. He constantly looks for alternative ways of expressing his essential concerns with an eye that looks beneath and beyond the surface of deserts, canyons, and clouds. An educator and artist, Tony is represented in galleries across the nation. Visitors to the Salt Lake International Airport are greeted by his enormous murals. These magnificent murals capture the essence of Utah's famous landmarks. A native Utahn, Tony received a master's of fine arts degree from the University of Utah in 1974. He was founding director of the Bountiful Art Center and has been on the faculties of Utah State University and the University of Utah. He is currently painting full time. We are proud to reproduce his art in the **Utah Celebrity and Local Heroes Cookbook***.*

Bryce Canyon National Park, Panel 2

Tony Rasmussen's work is available by writing:
Anton Rasmussen Prints, P.O. Box 58229, Salt Lake City, Utah 84158-0299.

thanks

photo credits

Thanks to each and every recipe contributor for taking the time, and showing you care.

To our friends at the Park City Performing Arts Center - especially Teri Orr, Mike Andrews and Ann MacQuoid.

Endless thanks to Sandra Hesselbacher for endless advice as our Recipe Editor.

The book wouldn't be the same without the art of Tony Rasmussen. Thanks for your generosity, Tony.

Very big thanks to Amy Funkhauser, our Business Manager and Sales Director.

For our beautiful and poetic design, Kim Woodland and Kristen Kopfer.

Our banker in cowboy boots, Andy Phillips, at West One Bank. Thanks, Andy.

Thanks to Keith Kampschror and Julie Driver for computer consulting.

Bill McMahan for guarding the fax machine and our sanity.

To our testing kitchen: Sandra Hesselbacher, Ruby Bleu, Sofia and Lucas Jaramillo, Ray Liermann, Sue Colyer, Linda Tawney, Shannon King, Connie Kirk, Ronda Cannon, and Millie Reid.

To our copyeditors: Rosemary Hardin, Rond Reid, Rosemary Kampschror, and Rick Hesselbacher.

For travel arrangements, John Kampschror.

Our ethnic food advisor, Rory Farrow.

Our expert in marketing and promotion, Nancy Kay.

For technical support, Bonnie Scudder.

For research, thanks to Peggy Stokes.

Helen Howard, for literary connections.

To Jonathan Hinckley, our printing wizard.

Our legal pro, thanks Harriet Parker Bass.

For celebrity information and expertise, continuous and immeasurable thanks to Robert J. Willert.

And special thanks to those who persevered and pestered friends and loved-ones for recipes and offered support and advice: Marilyn Andrews, Karen Avery, Kira Bailes, Patti Balli, Alison Barnett, Wendy Bower, Chapin Burke, Imogene Coca, Bill Cole, Velma Crown, Barbara Dunlea, Veronica Field, Pam Fogle, Larry Frederick, Ann Goddard, Lois Harmon, Roxanne Hasegawa, Don Heidel, Mindy Holland, Wendy Hopkins, Mardi Hudson, Bob Hunter, Carolyn Johnson, Becki Lewis, Marlene Luke, Lynn Mackey, Connie Marshall, Rosey Martenez, Scott Mason, Mark Menlove, Cindy Meyer, Camille Miner, Barbara Morris, Shelley Mortimer, Merrilee Muir, Amy Newman, Gerold Ottley, E.G. Perry, Rick Pollack, Dave Porter, Tina Quayle, Colleen Reardon, Jan Raio, Carmen Rogers, Tamarin Rose, Todd Schlopy, Caroline Shaw, Teresa Solorio, Chalise Smith, Shaun Stinsen, Pam Stucki, Shelley Thomas, Doug Thompson, Regis Tsosie, Johnny Unser, Nancy Volmer, Andrew Wallace, Stephanie Wanicur, Beth Wolfgram, Ginger Zanger.

order form

Please send the Utah Celebrity
& Local Heroes Cookbook to:

Ordered by

Name:_____
Address:_____
City:_____ State:_____
Zip:_____ Phone: (____)_____

Please send _____book(s)
at $20 each for a total of $_____

Plus Utah Sales Tax (as
appropriate depending
upon the county you reside in) $_____

Plus Shipping & Handling
at $3.00 per book for a total of $_____

TOTAL ENCLOSED: $_____

Please make checks payable to
the Park City Performing Arts Center.
Please do not send cash.
Sorry, no C.O.D.s.

Please charge my   ( ) Visa ( ) MasterCard

Credit Card number:_____
Expiration date:_____

Cardholder's
Signature:_____

Ship to (if other than the above address)
Name:_____
Address:_____
City:_____ State:_____
Zip:_____ Phone: (____)_____

All royalties benefit the Park City Performing
Arts Center.

Send to: Park City Performing Arts Center,
P.O. Box 1297, Park City, Utah, 84060.
(801) 655-8252

order form

Please send the Utah Celebrity
& Local Heroes Cookbook to:

Ordered by

Name:_____
Address:_____
City:_____ State:_____
Zip:_____ Phone: (____)_____

Please send _____book(s)
at $20 each for a total of $_____

Plus Utah Sales Tax (as
appropriate depending
upon the county you reside in) $_____

Plus Shipping & Handling
at $3.00 per book for a total of $_____

TOTAL ENCLOSED: $_____

Please make checks payable to
the Park City Performing Arts Center.
Please do not send cash.
Sorry, no C.O.D.s.

Please charge my   ( ) Visa ( ) MasterCard

Credit Card number:_____
Expiration date:_____

Cardholder's
Signature:_____

Ship to (if other than the above address)
Name:_____
Address:_____
City:_____ State:_____
Zip:_____ Phone: (____)_____

All royalties benefit the Park City Performing
Arts Center.

Send to: Park City Performing Arts Center,
P.O. Box 1297, Park City, Utah, 84060.
(801) 655-8252